Your Personal Bible

Your Personal Bible

Colin Urquhart

Hodder & Stoughton
LONDON SYDNEY AUCKLAND

First published in Great Britain 1994

10 9 8 7 6 5 4 3 2 1

ISBN 0 340 61243 6

Typeset by Hewer Text Composition Services, Edinburgh
Printed and bound in Great Britain by
Cox & Wyman, Reading, Berks

Hodder and Stoughton Ltd
A Division of Hodder Headline PLC
47 Bedford Square
London WC1B 3DP

To all those who want to live by the revelation of God's Word
and Truth found only in the Bible

Acknowledgments

My special thanks to my assistant, Paula, for the many hours spent in helping to prepare the material for this book, and to Samantha for her patient work on her word processor. I deeply appreciate all at Kingdom Faith who have supported me in prayer while writing this book. Caroline, my wife, has given her faithful love, support and encouragement and I am so grateful to the Lord for her. My thanks also for permission to use the New International Version Bible for the material in this book.

Contents

PART 4 COLLECTIONS OF SAYINGS ABOUT GOD AS YOUR FATHER: APPLYING THESE TRUTHS TO YOUR LIFE

PART 5 PERSONAL REVELATION OF TRUTH FROM THE EPISTLES

PART 7 PROMISES OF GOD FROM ISAIAH

PART 8 THE PSALMS AS PRAYER

PART 9 THE LORD SPEAKS DIRECTLY TO YOU THROUGH PROVERBS

PART 10 THE NAMES OF GOD

PART 11 SELECTIONS FROM REVELATION

FOREWORD

Receiving Revelation

It is wonderful that God has chosen to reveal himself to us as Father, Son and Holy Spirit. He has given us in the Bible the revelation of the truth about who he is, his nature and character. He has revealed in Scripture what he has done for us through Jesus in giving us salvation, making it possible for us to receive the gift of his kingdom and his life now. For it is only through Jesus Christ that we can know God personally.

The Holy Spirit guides us into all the truth of who God is and what he has done for us through Jesus. He takes the words of the Bible and brings them to life in our hearts, ensuring that we hear from God. And yet many Christians read the Bible without receiving the revelation of truth it contains; at least, not in a way that builds and encourages their faith. Many have never been taught how they can aid the process of revelation, how they can take hold of biblical truth and apply it to their own hearts and lives. This is not difficult to do when you know how. This book will help to make the Bible more personal for you. You will see how God can speak directly to you in a way that will encourage your faith and make an impact on your life.

During my thirty years of ministry as a pastor, preacher and teacher of God's Word, I have been concerned to learn how to enable others to grasp the wonderful truths of Scripture in such a way that they will hear God speaking to them personally and directly. In this book I am going to introduce you to a number of simple ways in which the Bible can mean more to you. I start from the premise that Jesus teaches us: if we continue in his words, we will be his disciples, we will know the truth and the truth will set us free.

The Bible is, then, the deposit of truth that God himself has provided for us and therefore needs to be central to the life of every believing Christian. For many years I have myself done exercises similar to those I outline in this book. Sometimes I write out passages of Scripture as they appear in the pages of the Bible. At other times I personalise the Scriptures so that God speaks the words directly to me. Or I write down in the first person singular, what the Word says to me about me. This has helped me, and many others I have taught, to identify personally with what is written in the Bible. This is not an attempt to change the Scriptures. God forbid! The Bible is such wonderful revelation of truth it could not in any way be improved upon. I want to make that absolutely clear. What is written in this book helps to bring out the meaning of the verses of Scripture for you personally. This book is intended to be a teaching aid to help you grow in faith as you receive personal revelation of the truth. Exercises such as these will intensify your love for the Bible and your dependence on the revelation of truth that it brings. God's Word will make an impact on your life in powerful ways, enabling you to live a more victorious Christian life.

My intention is that you should read these pages alongside the Bible text so that you can learn for yourself how to apply the truth to your own life. To help you do this the Scripture references are given for the various passages used. I want to encourage you to do similar exercises with the Scriptures yourself to see how this will stimulate your faith and enable you to walk in the truth. I have not attempted to cover the whole Bible, or even the whole of the New Testament. I have selected passages and references which will help you to see who you are in Christ and how you can overcome those things of self which are such a hindrance to the Christian life. The Bible is God's Word addressed to all sorts and conditions of men. There are passages of warning for rebellious opponents of truth; there are passages addressed to wayward believers living in disobedience; and there are passages spoken to and about faithful believers, those who want to honour God in their lives. For the most part this book concentrates on truths addressed to believers. At all times I have kept as close as possible to the biblical text. This is essential if you are to apply truth, rather than your own ideas, to your life. I have used the New International Version, but you can use in a similar way any version familiar to you.

Receiving revelation from the Bible is exciting. Every day I am excited when I sit down with my Bible because I know that God, the creator of heaven and earth, will speak to me personally. I can receive into my heart what is in his heart. I never cease to wonder at the privilege of this or the way that day by day God's Word makes an impact on my life.

HOW TO USE THIS BOOK

This book is divided into short sections so that you can use them devotionally on a daily basis, should you wish to do so. The biblical references for most passages are given, and I suggest that you read the biblical text either before or after reading one of the sections in this book. You can then see for yourself how close the section is to the original and how the scriptural truths are applied to you personally.

I have tried to arrange the material in a way that will help you to grow spiritually as you use it. You will see more of the wonderful truths of who you are in Christ because of all that he has done for you. You will grow in the understanding of the inheritance you have in him; and you will see how God has equipped you to walk in fellowship with him through the many dilemmas and difficulties we face in life. So the truths you discover in each section are to be appropriated by you. The truth is the same for every believer! So you are reading truths of what God has done for you personally!

In some Parts it will be simple to use the biblical text alongside the section from the book as all the references come from the same book of the Bible but in other Parts you will need to look up the references given as these are taken from different books of the Bible. However, the time spent doing this will prove worthwhile. You are handling truths that can have a deep impact on your life. For the truth of God's Word and the revelation we receive through Scripture are the only sure way of correcting our wrong concepts of who God is, of the purposes he has for our lives and how he views us as those who he has made alive in Christ. You will find that the Lord is far more loving, merciful and gracious to you than you are to yourself, or that you imagined he could be to you! That in itself is very encouraging.

Finally, let me once again urge you to do similar exercises with the Scriptures yourself. You will find this a great encouragement to your faith and will strengthen your personal relationship with your heavenly Father.

PART 1

Jesus Speaks Directly to You Through John's Gospel

Introduction

The Bible is God's written Word to you personally. Instead of writing down the truth about yourself, you can write it as if God is speaking directly to you. In this first Part we listen to Jesus speaking to us directly about himself, and about us as disciples. The truth is the same for all disciples of every generation. What Jesus taught those first disciples, he teaches us as his present-day disciples. Some passages are direct quotations from the biblical text. Other verses have been put in such a way that you can hear Jesus speaking to you personally. The truth of what he says has not been altered and will both build and challenge your faith. So, for example, the well-known passage from John 3:16–17 in the biblical text reads: 'For God so loved the world that he gave his one and only Son, that whoever believes in him shall not perish but have eternal life. For God did not send his Son into the world to condemn the world, but to save the world through him.' I have personalised this as follows: 'For my Father so loved the world that he gave me, his one and only Son, that whoever believes in me shall not perish but have eternal life. He did not send me into the world to condemn the world, but to save the world. Because you believe in me, you are not condemned, but whoever does not believe stands condemned already because he has not believed in my name, Jesus.'

You will find this a very helpful way of building your personal relationship with the Lord. As you become accustomed to him speaking personally to you through Scripture, so you will also become more sensitive to what he is saying to you through his Spirit. You become more in tune with his voice. This is a method I have used extensively for many years in my daily times with the Lord. There is no question that it has helped me immensely to receive the truth of Scripture personally and to strengthen my relationship with the Lord. There is great value in writing out passages of Scripture for yourself. Also it is good to speak them aloud as Jesus addressing his word personally to you.

1

The Word

———— ○ ————

In the beginning I existed, I was the Word, the Word that was with God, and the Word that is God. I was with God in the beginning. Through me all things were made; without me nothing was made that has been made. In me was life, and that life is your light. My light shines in the darkness, and the darkness has not understood it.

I am the true light that gives light to every man, and I came into the world. I was in the world, and though the world was made through me, the world did not recognise me. I came to that which was my own, but my own did not receive me. Yet to you who received me, who believed in my name, I gave the right to become a child of God – a child born not of natural descent, nor of human decision or a husband's will, but born of God.

I became flesh and made my dwelling with you. You have seen my glory, the glory of the One and Only, who came from the Father, full of grace and truth.

(John 1:1–5, 9–14)

2

The Kingdom of God

I tell you the truth, you can only see the kingdom of God because you have been born again.

I tell you the truth, no one can enter the kingdom of God unless he is born of water and the Spirit. Flesh gives birth to flesh, but the Spirit gives birth to spirit. You should not be surprised at my saying, 'You must be born again.' The wind blows wherever it pleases. You hear its sound, but you cannot tell where it comes from or where it is going. So it is with everyone born of the Spirit.

I, the Son of Man, had to be lifted up, that everyone who believes in me may have eternal life. For my Father so loved the world that he gave me, his one and only Son, that whoever believes in me shall not perish but have eternal life. He did not send me into the world to condemn the world, but to save the world. Because you believe in me, you are not condemned, but whoever does not believe stands condemned already because he has not believed in my name, Jesus.

This is the verdict: I came into the world as light, but men loved darkness instead of light because their deeds were evil. Everyone who does evil hates the light, and will not come into the light for fear that his deeds will be exposed. But you live by the truth and so you come into the light, so that it may be seen plainly that what you do you do through God.

(John 3:3, 5–8, 14–21)

3

The Holy Spirit

I speak the words of God, for I have the Spirit without limit. The Father loves me and has placed everything in my hands. Whoever believes in me has eternal life, but whoever rejects me will not see life, for my Father's wrath remains on him.

Everyone who drinks ordinary water will be thirsty again, but whoever drinks the water I give him will never thirst. Indeed, the water I give him will become in him a spring of water welling up to eternal life.

True worshippers worship my Father in spirit and truth, for they are the kind of worshippers he seeks. God is spirit, and his worshippers must worship in spirit and in truth.

The Spirit gives you life; your flesh counts for nothing. The words I have spoken to you are spirit and they are life. You can come to me only because the Father has enabled you.

I have given you the words of eternal life. You believe and know that I am the Holy One of God.

If you are thirsty, come to me and drink. When you believe in me, streams of living water will flow from within you. This is the life of the Spirit, whom you have received because you believe in me.

The Spirit of truth guides you into all truth. He does not speak on his own; he speaks only what he hears, and he tells you what is yet to come. He brings glory to me by taking from what is mine and making it known to you. All that belongs to the Father is mine. That is why I said the Spirit will take from what is mine and make it known to you.

Peace be with you! As the Father has sent me, I am sending you. Receive the Holy Spirit. If you forgive anyone his sins, they are forgiven; if you do not forgive them, they are not forgiven.

(John 3:34–6; 4:13–14, 23; 6:63, 64, 68–9; 7:37–9; 16:13–15; 20:21–3)

4

Jesus and the Father

My food is to do the will of him who sent me and to finish his work. Do you not say, 'Four months more and then the harvest'? I tell you, open your eyes and look at the fields! They are ripe for harvest. Even now the reaper draws his wages, even now he harvests the crop for eternal life, so that the sower and the reaper may be glad together. Thus the saying 'One sows and another reaps' is true. I sent you to reap what you have not worked for. Others have done the hard work, and you have reaped the benefits of their labour.

I tell you the truth, I can do nothing by myself; I can do only what I see my Father doing, because whatever the Father does I also do. For the Father loves me and shows me all he does. Yes, to your amazement I will show you even greater things than these. For just as the Father raises the dead and gives them life, even so, I give life to whom I am pleased to give it.

Moreover, the Father judges no one, but has entrusted all judgment to me, that all may honour me just as they honour the Father. He who does not honour me does not honour the Father, who sent me.

I tell you the truth, because you hear my word and believe him who sent me you have eternal life and will not be condemned; you have crossed over from death to life. I tell you the truth, a time is coming and has now come when the dead will hear the voice of the Son of God and those who hear will live. For as the Father has life in himself, so he has granted the Son to have life in himself. And he has given him authority to judge because he is the Son of Man.

Do not be amazed at this, for a time is coming when all who are in their graves will hear his voice and come out – those who have done good will rise to live, and those who have done evil will rise to be condemned.

By myself I can do nothing; I judge only as I hear, and my judgment is just, for I seek not to please myself but him who sent me.

(John 4:34–8; 5:19–30)

5

The Work my Father Requires

Beloved, do not work for food that spoils, but for food that endures to eternal life, which I give you. On you my Father has placed his seal of approval, because you believe in me. The work my Father requires of you is this – to believe in me!

My Father gives you the true bread from heaven. I am the bread of life. Because you come to me you will never go hungry, and because you believe in me you will never be thirsty. All that the Father gives me will come to me, and whoever comes to me I will never drive away. So I will never drive you away. For I came down from heaven not to do my will but to do the will of him who sent me. And this is the will of him who sent me, that I shall lose none of all that he has given me, but raise them up at the last day, including you. For my Father's will is that everyone who looks to me and believes me shall have eternal life, and I will raise him up at the last day.

You have come to me because the Father who sent me drew you, and I will raise you up at the last day. Everyone who listens to the Father and learns from him comes to me. I am the only one who has seen the Father. I tell you the truth, because you believe you have everlasting life.

I am the bread of life. But here is the bread that comes down from heaven, which you may eat and not die. I am the living bread that came down from heaven. If you eat of this bread, you will live for ever. This bread is my flesh, which I will give for the life of the world.

I tell you the truth, unless you can eat the flesh of the Son of Man and drink his blood, you have no life in you. Because you eat my flesh and drink my blood you have eternal life, and I will raise you up at the last day. For my flesh is real food and my blood is real drink. Because you eat my flesh and drink my blood you remain in me, and I in you. Just as the living Father sent me and I live because of the Father, so you feed on me and will live because of me. Because you feed on this bread you will live for ever.

(John 6:27, 29, 32, 35–40, 44–51, 53–8)

6

The Light of Life

I am the light of the world. When you follow me you will never walk in darkness, but will have the light of life.

Don't judge by human standards; I pass judgment on no one. But if I do judge, my decisions are right, because I am not alone. I stand with the Father, who sent me.

If you hold to my teaching, you are really my disciple. Then you will know the truth, and the truth will set you free.

I tell you the truth, everyone who sins is a slave to sin. Now a slave has no permanent place in the family, but a son belongs to it for ever. So if the Son sets you free, you will be free indeed.

Because you belong to me you hear what I say. I tell you the truth, if you keep my word, you will never see death. If you glorify yourself, your glory means nothing.

As long as it is day, you must do the work of him who sent me. Night is coming, when no one can work. While I am in the world, I am the light of the world.

(John 8:12, 15–16, 31–2, 34–6, 47, 51, 54; 9:4–5)

7

The Good Shepherd

I am the gate; because you enter through me you will be saved. You will come in and go out, and find pasture. The thief comes only to steal and kill and destroy; I have come that you may have life, and have it to the full.

I am the Good Shepherd. The Good Shepherd lays down his life for you as one of his sheep.

I am the Good Shepherd. I know you and you know me – just as the Father knows me and I know the Father – and I lay down my life for you. I have other sheep that are not of this sheep pen. I must bring them also. They too will listen to my voice, and there shall be one flock and one shepherd.

The reason my Father loves me is that I lay down my life – only to take it up again. No one takes it from me, but I lay it down of my own accord. I have authority to lay it down and authority to take it up again. This command I received from my Father.

You listen to my voice; I know you, and you follow me. I give you eternal life, and you shall never perish; no one can snatch you out of my hand. My Father, who has given you to me, is greater than all; no one can snatch you out of my Father's hand. I and the Father are one.

I am the resurrection and the life. Because you believe in me you will live, even though you die; and whoever lives and believes in me will never die. Do you believe this? You believe that I am the Christ, the Son of God, who was to come into the world.

(John 10:7–11, 14–18, 27–30; 11:25–7)

8

The Servant

I tell you the truth, unless a grain of wheat falls to the ground and dies, it remains only a single seed. But if it dies, it produces many seeds. If you love your life you will lose it, while if you hate your life in this world you will keep it for eternal life. To serve me you must follow me; and where I am, you as my servant also will be. My Father will honour you as you serve me.

I wash your feet. Often you do not realise what I am doing, but later you understand. Unless I wash you, you have no part with me.

You call me 'Teacher' and 'Lord', and rightly so, for that is what I am. Because I, your Lord and Teacher, wash your feet, you also should wash the feet of others. I have set you an example that you should do as I have done for you. I tell you the truth, no servant is greater than his master, nor is a messenger greater than the one who sent him. Now that you know these things, you will be blessed if you do them.

If you have my commands and obey them, you love me. If you love me you will be loved by my Father, and I too will love you and show myself to you. If you love me, you will obey my teaching. My Father will love you, and we will come to you and make our home with you. He who does not love me will not obey my teaching. These words you hear are not my own; they belong to the Father who sent me. The world must learn that I love the Father and that I do exactly what my Father has commanded me.

The Counsellor, the Holy Spirit, whom the Father sends in my name, teaches you all things and reminds you of everything I have said to you. Peace I leave with you; my peace I give you. I do not give to you as the world gives. Do not let your heart be troubled and do not be afraid.

(John 12:24–6; 13:5, 7–8, 13–17; 14:21, 23–4, 31, 26–7)

9

Abide in my Love

———— ○ ————

I am the true vine, and my Father is the gardener. He cuts off every branch in me that bears no fruit, while every branch that does bear fruit he prunes so that it will be even more fruitful. You are already clean because of the word I have spoken to you. Remain in me, and I will remain in you. No branch can bear fruit by itself; it must remain in the vine. Neither can you bear fruit unless you remain in me.

I am the vine; you are the branches. If a man remains in me and I in him, he will bear much fruit; apart from me you can do nothing. If anyone does not remain in me, he is like a branch that is thrown away and withers; such branches are picked up, thrown into the fire and burned. If you remain in me and my words remain in you, ask whatever you wish, and it will be given you. This is to my Father's glory, that you bear much fruit, showing yourself to be my disciple.

As the Father has loved me, so have I loved you. Now remain in my love. If you obey my commands, you will remain in my love, just as I have obeyed my Father's commands and remain in his love. I have told you this so that my joy may be in you and that your joy may be complete.

My command is this: 'Love others as I have loved you.' You can have no greater love than this, that you lay down your life for your friends. You are my friend if you do what I command. I no longer call you a servant, because a servant does not know his master's business. Instead, I have called you my friend, for everything that I learned from my Father I have made known to you. You did not choose me, but I chose you and appointed you to go and bear fruit – fruit that will last. Then the Father will give you whatever you ask in my name. This is my command: 'Love each other.'

I tell you the truth, my Father will give you whatever you ask in my name. Ask and you will receive, and your joy will be complete. The Father himself loves you because you have loved me and have believed that I came from God.

(John 15:1–8; 9–17; 16:23–4, 27)

10

Suffering and Glory

If the world hates you, keep in mind that it hated me first. If you belonged to the world, it would love you as its own. As it is, you do not belong to the world, but I have chosen you out of the world. That is why the world hates you.

Remember the words I spoke to you: 'No servant is greater than his master.' If they persecuted me, they will persecute you also. If they obeyed my teaching, they will obey yours also. They will treat you this way because of my name, for they do not know the one who sent me.

In this world you will have trouble. But take heart! I have overcome the world.

As the Father sent me into the world, I have sent you into the world. For your sake I sanctified myself, that you too may be truly sanctified.

I have given you the glory that the Father gave me, that you may be one with other believers as the Father and I are one. I want you to be in complete unity to let the world know that the Father sent me and has loved you even as he has loved me.

I want you who have been given me by my Father to be with me where I am, and to see my glory, the glory the Father has given me because he loved me before the creation of the world. I have made my Father known to you, and will continue to make him known in order that the love he has for me may be in you and that I myself may be in you.

(John 15:18–21; 16:33; 17:18, 22–4, 26)

PART 2

Main Themes: Collections of Verses in Personalised Form

Introduction

In this Part I have taken a number of central themes from the New Testament and brought together a number of verses relating to each theme from different books in the New Testament. You can do this yourself for other key words in the Bible by using a concordance and writing out the various Scriptures relating to those words. There are several computer programmes available now that do this for you. However, you will benefit far more by looking up and writing out these Scriptures for yourself.

The writing out of Bible verses helps concentration and understanding. It is also good to have to hand your own collection of verses that seem particularly relevant to you as a person, verses that the Lord has already used in your life in some particular way. You can read these at times when you feel under considerable pressure or in need.

Personalising the Verses

I have found great benefit from 'personalising' verses and passages from the Bible. I do this by writing them out in the first person singular, thus applying the truth to myself. I can receive these biblical truths as statements that relate to me personally. So, for example, in the N.I.V. text, Galatians 2:4–5 reads: 'But because of his great love for us, God, who is rich in mercy, made us alive with Christ even when we were dead in transgressions – it is by grace you have been saved.' It is a very simple matter to 'personalise' this so that I apply this great truth to myself: 'But because of his great love for me, God, who is rich in mercy, made me alive with Christ even when I was dead in transgressions – it is by grace I have been saved.' This is a truth about every born-again believer. It is, therefore, a truth for me to appropriate personally. This helps me to apply this truth to my own heart so that I may live in the good of it.

I have used a very simple example but sometimes you will find yourself faced with a statement that may challenge you. As you accept the truth for yourself so faith will rise in your heart. Let me give you an example of this. Hebrews 10:14 reads: 'Because by one sacrifice he has made perfect for ever those who are being made holy.' When you 'personalise' this it becomes: 'Because by one sacrifice he has made me perfect for ever because I am one who is being made holy.' Now you are faced with a great biblical truth, that as a born-again believer you are already made perfect for ever through the sacrifice of Jesus Christ. Do not be afraid to apply to yourself what the Bible says about you, even if you don't always understand how such statements could be true.

Many read these truths without applying them to themselves because they fail to see how they could possibly be true for them. Faith comes from hearing God's Word, by affirming it as the truth about you, no matter how you feel about yourself. We all have to learn to live by revelation of the truth instead of our own negative feelings or assessment of ourselves.

I have arranged the Scripture verses in each section in an order that will help you to understand the truth contained in them. I have avoided adding words of explanation, except in a few places. However, I have tried to place the material in each Part in a meaningful sequence. Issues opened up in one section will therefore be explained by material in subsequent sections. Sometimes I use the phrase 'including me' when I quote a corporate truth that I need to apply personally.

Please remember, we are not attempting to rewrite the Bible; we are learning to apply biblical truths to our lives, so that we can live and walk in the truth.

11
Saved

Jesus, the Son of Man, had to be lifted up on the cross so that I may have eternal life by believing in him. For God so loved the world that he gave his one and only Son, so that through believing in him I should not perish but have eternal life.

Because of his great love for me, God, who is rich in mercy, made me alive with Christ even when I was dead in transgressions – it is by grace I have been saved. And I also was included in Christ when I heard the word of truth, the gospel of my salvation. Having believed, I was marked in him with a seal, the promised Holy Spirit, who is a deposit guaranteeing my inheritance until the redemption of those who are God's possession to the praise of his glory.

Therefore, since I have been justified (made totally acceptable and righteous in God's sight) through faith, I have peace with God through my Lord Jesus Christ to whom I have gained access by faith into this grace in which I now stand. In him I have redemption through his blood, the forgiveness of my sins, in accordance with the riches of God's grace that he lavished on me with all wisdom and understanding.

Because I believe that Jesus is the Christ I am born of God. Though I have not seen him I love him; and even though I do not see him now, I believe in him and am filled with an inexpressible and glorious joy, for I am receiving the goal of my faith, the salvation of my soul.

(John 3:14–16; Eph. 2:4–5; 1:13–14; Rom. 5:1–2; Eph. 1:7–8; 1 John 5:1; 1 Pet. 8–9)

12

Chosen

Because I acknowledge that Jesus is the Son of God, God lives in me and I in God. I know that I live in him and he in me, because he has given me of his Spirit. Therefore, because I am in Christ, I am a new creation; the old has gone, the new has come! If I remain in Jesus and he in me, I will bear much fruit. Apart from him I can do nothing.

In Christ all the fullness of the Deity lives in bodily form, and I have been given fullness in Christ, who is the Head over every power and authority. In him I have been enriched in every way – in all my speaking and in all my knowledge.

In love he predestined me to be adopted as his son through Jesus Christ in accordance with his pleasure and will – to the praise of his glorious grace, which is freely given me in the one he loves. And God raised me up with Christ and seated me with him in the heavenly realms in Christ Jesus, in order that in the coming ages he might show the incomparable riches of his grace, expressed in his kindness to me in Christ Jesus. For it is by grace I have been saved through faith – and this is not from myself, it is the gift of God – not by works, so that I cannot boast.

Blessed be the God and Father of my Lord Jesus Christ, who has blessed me in Christ with every spiritual blessing in the heavenly realms.

All this is from God, who reconciled me to himself through Christ and gave me the ministry of reconciliation: that God was reconciling the world to himself in Christ, not counting my sins against me. And he has committed to me the message of reconciliation. For he chose me in him before the creation of the world to be holy and blameless in his sight. For I am God's workmanship, created in Christ Jesus to do good works, which God prepared in advance for me to do.

(1 John 4:15, 13; 2 Cor. 5:17; John 15:5; Col. 2:9–10; 1 Cor. 1:4–5; Eph. 1:4–6; 2:6–9; 1:3; 2 Cor. 5:18–19; Eph. 2:10)

13

Grace

Grace and peace are mine from God my Father and from the Lord Jesus Christ. I am justified (made acceptable) freely by his grace through the redemption that came by Christ Jesus. Because I have received God's abundant provision of grace, and the gift of righteousness, I will reign in life through the one man, Jesus Christ.

By the grace of God I am what I am, and his grace to me was not without effect. By faith I have gained access into this grace in which I now stand. I have not received God's grace in vain.

I know the grace of my Lord Jesus Christ, that though he was rich, yet for my sake he became poor, so that I through his poverty might become rich. And God is able to make all grace abound to me, so that in all things at all times, having all that I need, I will abound in every good work. I am to excel in the grace of giving.

From the fullness of his grace, I have received one blessing after another. Through his grace I have been enriched in every way – in all my speaking and in all my knowledge. I have gifts according to the grace given to me.

God's grace is sufficient for me, for his power is made perfect in weakness. He has freely given me his glorious grace in the one he loves. But to each one of us grace has been given as Christ apportioned it.

I can approach the throne of grace with confidence, so that I may receive mercy and find grace to help me in my time of need. I set my life fully on the grace to be given me when Jesus Christ is revealed.

(Rom. 1:7; 3:24; 5:17; 1 Cor. 15:10; Rom. 5:2; 2 Cor. 6:1; 8:9; 9:8; 8:7; John 1:16; 1 Cor. 1:5; Rom. 12:6; 2 Cor. 12:9; Eph. 1:6; 4:7; Heb. 4:16; 1 Pet. 1:13)

14

More Grace

In him I have redemption through his blood, the forgiveness of my sins, in accordance with the riches of God's grace that he lavished on me with all wisdom and understanding. For it is by grace I have been saved, through faith – and this is not from myself, it is the gift of God – not by works, so that I cannot boast.

The grace of my Lord Jesus was poured out on me abundantly, along with the faith and love that are in Christ Jesus. This grace was given to me in Christ Jesus before the beginning of time, but it has now been revealed through the appearing of my Saviour, Christ Jesus, who has destroyed death and has brought life and immortality to light through the gospel. By his grace God has given me eternal encouragement and good hope, encouraging my heart and strengthening me in every good deed and word. I am to be strong in the grace that is in Christ Jesus.

By the grace of God Jesus tasted death for everyone – including me! Having been justified by his grace, I became his heir, having the hope of eternal life. It is good for my heart to be strengthened by grace. Grace and peace are mine in abundance.

For the grace of God that brings salvation has appeared to all men. It teaches us to say 'No' to ungodliness and worldly passions, and to live self-controlled, upright and godly lives in this present age, while we wait for the blessed hope – the glorious appearing of our great God and Saviour, Jesus Christ, who gave himself for us to redeem us from all wickedness and to purify for himself a people that are his very own, eager to do what is good. The gospel is growing and bearing fruit in me since the day I heard it and understood God's grace in all its truth.

I should use whatever gift I have received to serve others, faithfully administering God's grace in its various forms. God opposes the proud but gives grace to the humble.

The God of all grace, who called me to his eternal glory in Christ, after I have suffered a little while, will himself restore me and make me strong, firm and steadfast.

(Eph. 1:7–8; 2:8–9; 1 Tim. 1:14; 2 Tim. 1:9–10; 2 Thess. 2:16; 2 Tim. 2:1; Heb. 2:9; Titus 3:7; Heb. 13:9; 1 Pet. 1:2; Titus 2:11–14; Col. 1:6; 1 Pet. 4:10; Jas. 4:6; 1 Pet. 5:10)

15

The Precious Blood of Jesus

———— ○ ————

Blood and water flowed from Jesus's side for me! 'This is my blood of the (new) covenant, which is poured out for many for the forgiveness of sins.' That blood was poured out for my forgiveness. I share in the cup of the new covenant in Jesus's blood; whenever I drink it, I do so in remembrance of him. I am not to eat the bread or drink the cup of the Lord in an unworthy manner or I will be guilty of sinning against the body and blood of the Lord.

Jesus said that unless I eat the flesh of the Son of Man and drink his blood, I have no life in me. I will therefore feed on him in every way he makes himself available to me. Jesus said that if I eat his flesh and drink his blood I will have eternal life, and he will raise me up at the last day. His flesh is real food and his blood is real drink. If I eat his flesh and drink his blood I remain in him, and he in me.

Jesus is the sacrifice of atonement. My sins are atoned for and I am put right with God through faith in his blood. In Jesus I have redemption through his blood, the forgiveness of my sins, in accordance with the riches of God's grace. I have now been justified by his blood; how much more shall I be saved from God's wrath through him!

Now in Christ Jesus I who once was far away have been brought near to him through the blood of Christ. I have confidence to enter the most holy place by the blood of Jesus. Through Jesus God reconciles to himself all things, whether things on earth or things in heaven, by making peace through his blood, shed on the cross.

(John 19:34; Matt. 26:28; 1 Cor. 11:25, 27; John 6:53–6; Rom. 3:25; Eph. 1:7; Rom. 5:9; Eph. 2:13; Heb. 10:19; Col. 1:20)

16

Cleansed by the Blood

Jesus entered the most holy place once for all by his own blood, having obtained eternal redemption. The blood of Christ, who through the eternal Spirit offered himself unblemished to God, cleanses my conscience from acts that lead to death, so that I may serve the living God!

Without the shedding of Jesus's blood there is no forgiveness. I am made holy through Jesus's own blood. The God of peace brought Jesus back from the dead through the blood of the eternal covenant. I am part of that covenant by his grace.

I have been chosen according to the foreknowledge of God the Father, through the sanctifying work of the Spirit, for obedience to Jesus Christ and sprinkling by his blood. Grace and peace are mine in abundance. I have been redeemed with the precious blood of Christ, a lamb without blemish or defect.

If I walk in the light, as he is in the light, I have fellowship with others, and the blood of Jesus, God's Son, purifies me from all my sin. Jesus loves me and has freed me from my sins by his blood. With his blood, Jesus purchased men for God from every tribe and language and people and nation. He purchased me for God with his blood.

I am able to overcome my accuser by the blood of the Lamb and by the word of my testimony.

(Heb. 9:12, 14, 22; 13:12, 20; 1 Pet. 1:2, 19; 1 John 1:7; Rev. 1:5; 5:9; 12:11)

17

The Cross

Unless I take up my cross and follow Jesus I am not worthy of him. To follow Jesus, I must deny myself and take up my cross and follow him. If I do not carry my cross and follow Jesus I cannot be his disciple.

When I preach the gospel it is not to be with words of human wisdom, lest the cross of Christ be emptied of its power. For the message of the cross is foolishness to those who are perishing, but to me as one who is being saved it is the power of God. The cross is an offence to those who live by religious law. Many live as enemies of the cross of Christ.

Through the cross God reconciles us to himself and puts to death the hostility between us. May I never boast except in the cross of our Lord Jesus Christ, through which the world has been crucified to me, and I to the world.

And being found in appearance as a man, Jesus humbled himself and became obedient to death – even death on a cross!

Through Jesus God has chosen to reconcile to himself all things, whether things on earth or things in heaven, by making peace through his blood, shed on the cross.

God has made me alive with Christ. He forgave me all my sins having cancelled the written code, with its regulations, that was against me and that stood opposed to me; he took it away, nailing it to the cross.

I fix my eyes on Jesus, the author and perfecter of my faith, who for the joy set before him endured the cross, scorning its shame, and sat down at the right hand of the throne of God. And having disarmed the powers and authorities, he made a public spectacle of them, triumphing over them by the cross.

I have been crucified with Christ and I no longer live, but Christ lives in me. The life I live in the body, I live by faith in the Son of God, who loved me and gave his life for me. I do not set aside the grace of God, for if righteousness could be gained through the law, Christ died for nothing!

(Matt. 10:38; 16:24; Luke 14:27; 1 Cor. 1:17–18; Gal. 5:11; Phil. 3:18; Eph. 2:16; Gal. 6:14; Phil. 2:8; Col. 1:20; 2:13–15; Heb. 12:12; Col. 2:15; Gal. 2:20–1)

18

'Have Mercy, Lord'

I pray to my heavenly Father: Hear my cry for mercy as I call to you for help, as I lift up my hands towards your most holy place. Do not withhold your mercy from me, O Lord; may your love and truth always protect me. I said, 'O Lord, have mercy on me; heal me, for I have sinned against you.'

Have mercy on me, O God, according to your unfailing love; according to your great compassion blot out my transgressions. Have mercy on me, O God, have mercy on me, for in you my soul takes refuge. I will take refuge in the shadow of your wings until the disaster has passed. Answer me, O Lord, out of the goodness of your love; in your great mercy turn to me.

Have mercy on me, O Lord, for I call to you all day long. Hear my prayer, O Lord, listen to my cry for mercy. Turn to me and have mercy on me, as you always do to those who love your name. O Lord, hear my voice. Let your ears be attentive to my cry for mercy. O Lord, hear my prayer, listen to my cry for mercy; in your faithfulness and righteousness come to my relief. O Lord, I say to you, 'You are my God.' Hear, O Lord, my cry for mercy. Jesus, Son of David, have mercy on me!

I love you, Lord, for you heard my voice; you heard my cry for mercy. To you, O Lord, I called; to the Lord I cried for mercy.

Mercy triumphs over judgment! Mercy, peace and love are mine in abundance.

(Ps. 28:2; 40:11; 41:4; 51:1; 57:1; 69:16; 86:3; 86:6; 119:132; 103:2; 143:1; 140:6; Mark 10:47; Ps. 116:1; 30:8; Jas. 2:13; Jude 1:2)

19

God's Mercy

I am blessed when I am merciful, for I will be shown mercy. I should have mercy on others just as the Lord has mercy on me. When I show mercy, I am to do so cheerfully. I want to tell others how much the Lord has done for me, and how he has had mercy on me.

His mercy extends to me because I fear him. In view of God's mercy, I offer my body as a living sacrifice, holy and pleasing to God – this is my spiritual act of worship. God is rich in mercy towards me. Grace, mercy and peace are mine from God the Father and Christ Jesus my Lord.

He saved me, not because of righteous things I had done, but because of his mercy. The Lord is full of mercy and compassion towards me. In his great mercy he has given me new birth into a loving hope through the resurrection of Jesus Christ from the dead. Once I had not received mercy, but now I have received mercy.

I keep myself in God's love as I wait for the mercy of my Lord Jesus Christ to bring me to eternal life. I approach the throne of grace with confidence, so that I may receive mercy and find grace to help me in my time of need.

(Matt. 5:7; 18:33; Rom. 12:8; Mark 5:19; Luke 1:50; Rom. 12:1; Eph. 2:4; 1 Tim. 1:2; Titus 3:5; Jas. 5:11; 1 Pet. 1:3; 2:10; Jude 1:21; Heb. 4:16)

20

My Inheritance

My Father's will is that if I look to the Son and believe in him, I shall have eternal life, and I will be raised up at the last day.

I praise my God and Father and my Lord Jesus Christ! In his great mercy he has given me new birth into a living hope through the resurrection of Jesus Christ from the dead, and into an inheritance that can never perish, spoil or fade – kept in heaven for me, who through faith am shielded by God's power until the coming of the salvation that is ready to be revealed in the last time. Here is a trustworthy saying: if I died with him I will also live with him; if I endure, I will also reign with him. If I disown him, he also will disown me; if I am faithless he will remain faithful, for he cannot disown himself.

As in Adam I die, so in Christ I am made alive. Now I am a child of God and what I will be has not yet been made known. But I know that when he appears I shall be like him, for I shall see him as he is. When Christ who is my life appears, then I also will appear with him in glory.

Christ was sacrificed once to take away my sins; and he will appear a second time, not to bear sin, but to bring salvation to me and others who are waiting for him.

And surely you will be with me always, to the very end of the age. Never will you leave me; never will you forsake me. So I can say with confidence, I will not be afraid. What can man do to me?

I am to be joyful always; to pray continually; I am to give thanks in all circumstances, for this is God's will for me in Christ Jesus.

Through Jesus, therefore, I will continually offer to God a sacrifice of praise – the fruit of lips that confess his name. And I will not forget to do good and to share with others, for with such sacrifices God is pleased.

(John 6:40; 1 Pet. 1:3–5; 2 Tim. 2:11–13; 1 Cor. 15:22; 1 John 3:2; Col. 3:4; Heb. 9:28; Matt. 28:20; Heb. 13:5–6; 1 Thess. 5:16–18; Heb. 13:15–16)

21

I Have Died

I have been crucified with Christ, and I no longer live, but Christ lives in me. The life I live in the body, I live by faith in the Son of God, who loved me and gave himself for me. Now if I died with Christ, I believe I will also live with him.

When I was baptised in Christ Jesus, I was baptised into his death. I was therefore buried with him through baptism into death in order that, just as Christ was raised from the dead through the glory of the Father, I too may live a new life. For I know that my old self was crucified with him so that the body of sin may be rendered powerless, that I should no longer be a slave to sin – because if I have died I have been freed from sin.

May I never boast except in the cross of my Lord Jesus Christ, through which the world has been crucified to me, and I to the world. I died with Christ to the basic principles of this world. I also died to the (religious) law through the body of Christ, that I might belong to another, to him who was raised from the dead, in order that I might bear fruit for God. For I died, and my life is now hidden with Christ in God.

(Gal. 2:20; Rom. 6:8, 3–4, 6–7; Gal. 6:14; Col. 2:20; Rom. 7:4; Col. 3:3)

22

Jesus Loves Me

Jesus loves me as his own and has shown me the full extent of his love. God demonstrates his own love for me in this – while I was still a sinner, Christ died for me. Jesus has made the Father known to me, and will continue to make him known in order that the love the Father has for Jesus may be in me and that Jesus himself may be in me.

As the Father has loved Jesus, so has he loved me. Now I can remain in his love. If I obey his commands, I will remain in his love, just as he obeyed his Father's commands and remained in his love. If I love Jesus, I will obey his teaching. His Father will love me, and they will come to me and make their home with me.

Jesus's command to me is this: I am to love others as he has loved me. I can have no greater love than this, that I lay down my life for my friends. This is his command: I am to love others. If I love those who love me, what credit is that to me? Even 'sinners' love those who love them. I am to love my enemies, to do good to those who hate me. I am to love my enemies, to do good to them, and to lend to them without expecting to get anything back. Then my reward will be great, and I will be a son of the Most High, because he is kind to the ungrateful and wicked.

I am to love the Lord my God with all my heart and with all my soul and with all my mind. I cannot serve two masters. Either I will hate the one and love the other, or I will be devoted to the one and despise the other. I cannot serve both God and money.

(John 13:1; Rom. 5:8; John 17:26; 15:9–10; 14:23; 15:12–13, 17; Luke 6:32, 27, 35; Matt. 22:37; Luke 16:13)

23

Loving Others

Though I have not seen him, I love him; and even though I do not see him now, I believe in him and am filled with an inexpressible and glorious joy. Now that I have purified myself by obeying the truth so that I have sincere love for my brothers, I love others deeply, from the heart. I live in harmony with others; I am sympathetic, I love as a brother, I am compassionate and humble. Above all, I love others deeply, because love covers over a multitude of sins.

If I obey his word, God's love is truly made complete in me.

How great is the love the Father has lavished on me, that I should be called a child of God! And that is what I am! The reason the world does not know me is that it did not know him. I know that I have passed from death to life, because I love my brothers. Anyone who does not love remains in death.

This is how I know what love is: Jesus Christ laid down his life for me. And I ought to lay down my life for my brothers. If I have material possessions and see my brother in need but have no pity on him, how can the love of God be in me? I do not love with words or tongue but with actions and in truth. And this is his command: to believe in the name of his Son, Jesus Christ, and to love others as he commanded me.

This is love: not that I loved God, but that he loved me and sent his Son as an atoning sacrifice for my sins. Since God so loved me, I also ought to love others. If I love others, God lives in me and his love is made complete in me. I am to love others, for love comes from God. Everyone who loves has been born of God and knows God. Whoever does not love does not know God, because God is love.

(1 Pet. 1:8, 22; 3:8; 4:8; 1 John 2:5; 3:1, 14, 16–18, 23; 4:10–12, 7–8)

24

Increasing Love

Jesus has given me a new command. I am to love others. As he has loved me, so I must love others. By this all men will know that I am his disciple, if I love others. If I love Jesus, I will obey what he commands. By having Jesus's commands and obeying them, I am one who loves him. Because I love Jesus I will be loved by my Father, and Jesus, too, will love me and show himself to me. Nothing in all creation will be able to separate me from the love of God that is in Christ Jesus, my Lord.

Christ's love compels me, because I am convinced that he died for me. The grace of the Lord Jesus Christ, and the love of God, the fellowship of the Holy Spirit is with me.

I pray that I, being rooted and established in love, have power, together with all the saints, to grasp how wide and long and high and deep is the love of Christ, and to know this love that surpasses knowledge – that I may be filled to the measure of all the fullness of God.

May the Lord make my love increase and overflow for others. May the Lord direct my heart into God's love and Christ's perseverance. The goal of God's command is love, which comes from a pure heart and a good conscience and a sincere faith.

If I speak in the tongues of men and of angels, but have not love, I am only a resounding gong or a clanging cymbal. If I have the gift of prophecy and can fathom all mysteries and all knowledge, and if I have a faith that can move mountains, but have not love, I am nothing. If I give all I possess to the poor and surrender my body to the flames, but have not love, I gain nothing.

Love is patient, love is kind. It does not envy, it does not boast, it is not proud. Love does not delight in evil but rejoices in the truth. Love never fails. And now these three remain: faith, hope and love. But the greatest of these is love. I am to follow the way of love and eagerly desire spiritual gifts, especially the gift of prophecy. I am to do everything in love. The only thing that counts is faith expressing itself through love.

(John 13:34; 14:15, 21; Rom. 8:39; 2 Cor. 5:14; 13:14; Eph. 3:17–19; 1 Thess. 3:12; 2 Thess. 3:5; 1 Tim. 1:5; 1 Cor. 13:1–4, 6, 8, 13; 14:1, 16:14; Gal. 5:6)

25

Sincere Love

I was called to be free. I do not use my freedom to indulge the flesh; but, rather, to serve others in love. I am to be completely humble and gentle; to be patient, bearing with others in love.

I live a life of love, just as Christ loved me and gave himself up for me as a fragrant offering and sacrifice to God. May the Lord make my love increase and overflow for others. May the Lord direct my heart into God's love and Christ's perseverance.

My love must be sincere. I hate what is evil; I cling to what is good. I am devoted to others in brotherly love. I honour others above myself.

I am to let no debt remain outstanding, except the continuing debt to love others, for if I love my fellow man I have fulfilled the law. If I love, I do no harm to my neighbour. Therefore, love is the fulfilment of the law. If my brother is distressed because of what I eat, I am no longer acting in love.

I pray that my love may abound more and more. I am to set an example for the believers in speech, in life, in love, in faith and in purity. God did not give me a spirit of timidity, but a spirit of power, of love and of self-discipline.

Knowledge puffs up, but love builds up. Love with faith came from God the Father and the Lord Jesus Christ. His grace comes to me as I love my Lord Jesus Christ with an undying love.

By speaking the truth in love, I will in all things grow up into him who is my Head, that is, Christ. Has not God chosen me who am poor in the eyes of the world to be rich in faith and to inherit the kingdom he promised those who love him?

(Gal. 5:13; Eph. 4:2; 5:2; 1 Thess. 3:12; 2 Thess. 3:5; Rom. 12:9–10; 13:8, 10; 14:15; Phil. 1:9; 1 Tim. 4:12; 2 Tim. 1:7; 1 Cor. 8:1; Eph. 6:23–4; 4:15; Jas. 2:5)

26

I Love God

I know and rely on the love God has for me. God is love. Because I live in love I live in God, and God in me. In this way, love is made complete among us so that we will have confidence on the day of judgment, because in this world we are like him.

There is no fear in love. But perfect love drives out fear, because fear has to do with punishment. The one who fears is not made perfect in love. I love because he first loved me. If I say, 'I love God' yet hate my brother, I am a liar. For if I do not love my brother, whom I have seen, I cannot love God, whom I have not seen. He has given me this command – because I love God I must also love my brother.

This is how I know that I love the children of God: by loving God and carrying out his commands. This is how I love God: I obey his commands. And his commands are not burdensome.

I do not love the world or anything in the world. If I loved the world, the love of the Father would not be in me. If I belonged to the world, it would love me as its own. As it is, I do not belong to the world, but Jesus has chosen me out of the world. That is why the world hates me. I am to keep my life free from the love of money and be content with what I have, because God has said, 'Never will I leave you; never will I forsake you.'

This is love: that I walk in obedience to his commands. As I have heard from the beginning, his command is that I walk in love. I am to love others in the truth. I should consider how I may spur others on towards love and good deeds. Mercy, peace and love are mine in abundance.

Hope does not disappoint me, because God has poured out his love into my heart by the Holy Spirit, whom he has given me.

And I know that in all things God works for my good because I love him, and have been called according to his purpose.

(1 John 4:16–21; 5:2–3, 15; John 15:19; Heb. 13:5; 2 John 1:6; 3 John 1:1; Heb. 10:24; Jude 1:2; Rom. 5:5; 8:28)

27

Set Free

There is now no condemnation for me because I am in Christ Jesus, because through Christ Jesus the law of the Spirit of life set me free from the law of sin and death. By the free gift of God's grace I am put right with him through Christ Jesus, who has set me free. I have freedom in Christ Jesus.

God has made me alive with Christ. He forgave me all my sins, having cancelled the written code, with its regulations, that was against me and that stood opposed to me; he took it away, nailing it to the cross. And having disarmed the powers and authorities, he made a public spectacle of them, triumphing over them by the cross. For Christ died for sins once for all, the righteous for the unrighteous to bring me to God. He was put to death in the body but made alive by the Spirit.

This is love, not that I loved God but that he loved me and sent his son as an atoning sacrifice for my sins. When I turned to the Lord the veil separating me from God was taken away. Now the Lord is the Spirit, and where the Spirit of the Lord is there is freedom.

He too shared in our humanity, so that by his death he might destroy him who holds the power of death – that is, the devil – and free me from being held in slavery by the fear of death.

He entered heaven itself, now to appear for me in God's presence. He is able to save me completely because I have come to God through him, and he always lives to intercede for me. Such a high priest meets my need – one who is holy, blameless, pure, set apart from sinners, exalted above the heavens. Jesus suffered to make me holy through his own blood.

(Rom. 8:1–2; 3:26–GNB; Col. 2:13–15; 1 Pet. 3:18; 1 John 4:10; 2 Cor. 3:16–17; Heb. 2:14–15; 9:24; 7:25–6; 13:12)

28

Filled with Power

———— ○ ————

I have received what my Father promised; I have been clothed with power from on high. I received power when the Holy Spirit came on me; and I am Jesus's witness.

I am not ashamed of the gospel, because it is the power of God for the salvation of everyone who believes. For the kingdom of God is not a matter of talk but of power. I have been given authority to overcome all the power of the enemy; nothing will harm me. As a believer Jesus gave me power and authority to drive out all demons and to cure diseases. The weapons I fight with are not the weapons of the world. On the contrary, they have divine power to demolish strongholds.

'My grace is sufficient for you, for my power is made perfect in weakness.' Therefore, I will boast all the more gladly about my weaknesses, so that Christ's power may rest on me. But I have this treasure in a jar of clay to show that this all-surpassing power is from God and not from me.

God has given his incomparably great power to me because I believe. That power is like the working of his mighty strength, which he exerted in Christ when he raised him from the dead. He is able to do immeasurably more than all I ask or imagine, according to his power that is at work within me.

For the message of the cross is foolishness to those who are perishing, but to us who are being saved it is the power of God. God has power to do what he has promised me. My Holy Father protects me by the power of his name – the name he gave Jesus.

(Luke 24:49; Acts 1:8; Rom. 1:16; 1 Cor. 4:20; Luke 10:19; 9:1; 2 Cor. 10:4; 12:9; 4:7; Eph. 1:19–20; 3:20; 1 Cor. 1:18; Rom. 4:21; John 17:11)

29

In the Power of the Spirit

For to be sure, he was crucified in weakness, yet he lives by God's power. Likewise, I am weak in him, yet by God's power I will live with him to serve others. I pray that out of his glorious riches he may strengthen me with power through his Spirit in my inner being that I may have power, together with all the saints, to grasp how wide and long and high and deep is the love of Christ.

I will be strong in the Lord and in his mighty power. I have been given fullness in Christ, who is the head over every power and authority. I have been buried with him in baptism and raised with him through my faith in the power of God, who raised him from the dead.

I pray that I might be strengthened with all power according to his glorious might so that I may have great endurance and patience, and joyfully give thanks to the Father, who has qualified me to share in the inheritance of the saints in the kingdom of light.

By his power God raised the Lord from the dead, and he will raise me also. My body is sown in weakness, it is raised in power.

Through faith I am shielded by God's power until the coming of the salvation that is ready to be revealed in the last time. I want to know Christ and the power of his resurrection.

His divine power has given me everything I need for life and godliness through my knowledge of him who called me by his own glory and goodness. I am to spread the gospel not simply with words, but also with power, with the Holy Spirit and with deep conviction. For God did not give me a spirit of timidity, but a spirit of power, of love and of self-discipline.

I pray that God may count me worthy of his calling, and that by his power he may fulfil every good purpose of mine and every act prompted by my faith. May the God of hope fill me with all joy and peace as I trust in him, so that I may overflow with hope by the power of the Holy Spirit.

My message and my preaching are not to be with wise and persuasive words, but with a demonstration of the Spirit's power, so that people's faith might not rest on my wisdom, but on God's power.

(2 Cor. 13:4; Eph. 3:16–18; 6:10; Col. 2:10, 12; 1:11; 1 Cor. 6:14; 15:43; 1 Pet. 1:5; Phil. 3:10; 2 Pet. 1:3; 1 Thess. 1:5; 2 Tim. 1:7; 2 Thess. 1:11; Rom. 15:13; 1 Cor. 2:4–5)

30

Peace with God

Jesus says to me: 'Peace I leave with you; my peace I give you. I do not give to you as the world gives. Do not let your heart be troubled and do not be afraid. I have told you these things, so that in me you may have peace. In this world you will have trouble. But take heart! I have overcome the world.' For the kingdom of God is not a matter of eating and drinking, but of righteousness, peace and joy in the Holy Spirit.

Since I have been justified through faith, I have peace with God through my Lord Jesus Christ. Grace and peace are mine from God my Father and from the Lord Jesus Christ. May the God of hope fill me with all joy and peace as I trust in him, so that I may overflow with hope by the power of the Holy Spirit. The mind of sinful man is death, but the mind controlled by the Spirit is life and peace.

May the God of peace, who through the blood of the eternal covenant brought back from the dead our Lord Jesus, that great Shepherd of the sheep, equip me with every good thing for doing his will, and may he work in me what is pleasing to him, through Jesus Christ, to whom be glory for ever and ever. Amen. The God of peace will soon crush Satan under my feet.

The peace of God, which transcends all understanding, will guard my heart and my mind in Christ Jesus. Grace and peace are mine in abundance through the knowledge of God and of Jesus my Lord.

(John 14:27; 16:33; Rom. 14:17; 5:1; 1:7; 15:13; 8:6; Heb. 13:20–1; Rom. 16:20; Phil. 4:7; 2 Pet. 1:2)

31

He is my Peace

As far as it is possible, as far as it depends on me, I live at peace with everyone. I am to make every effort to do what leads to peace and to mutual edification. God has called me to live in peace. I am to live in peace. And the God of love and peace is with me. For God is not a God of disorder but of peace.

For he himself is my peace. I make every effort to keep the unity of the Spirit through the bond of peace. The peace of Christ is to rule in my heart, since as a member of his body I am called to peace. Now may the Lord of peace himself give me peace at all times and in every way.

May God himself, the God of peace, sanctify me through and through. May my whole spirit, soul and body be kept blameless at the coming of our Lord Jesus Christ. The God of peace is with me. Amen.

I make every effort to live in peace with all men and to be holy; without holiness I will not see the Lord. I am to flee the evil desires of youth, and pursue righteousness, faith, love and peace, along with those who call on the Lord out of a pure heart. I must turn from evil and do good; I must seek peace and pursue it.

No discipline seems pleasant at the time, but painful. Later on, however, it produces a harvest of righteousness and peace in me because I have been trained by it. Peacemakers who sow in peace raise a harvest of righteousness. I make every effort to be found spotless, blameless and at peace with him.

Peace to all who are in Christ.

(Rom. 12:18; 14:19; 1 Cor. 7:15; 2 Cor. 13:11; 1 Cor. 14:33; Eph. 2:14; 4:3; Col. 3:15; 2 Thess. 3:16; 1 Thess. 5:23; Rom. 15:33; Heb. 12:14; 2 Tim. 2:22; Heb. 12:11; Jas. 3:18; 2 Pet. 3:14; 1 Pet. 5:14)

32

The Heart

I am blessed if I have a pure heart, for this will enable me to see God. I am yoked with Jesus and learn from him, for he is gentle and humble in heart, and I will find rest for my soul. Jesus encourages me to take heart, for he forgives my sins and heals me!

Those with hard hearts do not hear with their ears, and they have closed their eyes to the truth. If they saw with their eyes, and heard with their ears, they would understand with their hearts and turn, and the Lord would heal them. When anyone hears the message about the kingdom and does not understand it, the evil one comes and snatches away what was sown in his heart. This is the seed sown along the path. But the things that come out of the mouth come from the heart, and these make a man 'unclean'. For out of the heart come evil thoughts, murder, adultery, sexual immorality, theft, false testimony, and slander.

Those with stubborn and unrepentant hearts are storing up wrath against themselves for the day of God's wrath, when his righteous judgment will be revealed.

The good man brings good things out of the good stored up in his heart, and the evil man brings evil things out of the evil stored up in his heart. For out of the overflow of my heart my mouth speaks.

I am to love the Lord my God with all my heart and with all my soul and with all my mind. Where my treasure is, there my heart is.

The Lord knows my heart. I want to be a person after God's own heart! Then I will do everything he wants me to do.

God, who knows my heart, has shown that he accepted me by giving the Holy Spirit to me. The seed on good soil stands for those with a noble and good heart, who hear the word, retain it, and by persevering produce a crop. My life is to be good soil.

The Word is near me; it is in my mouth and in my heart, the Word of faith proclaimed to me. If I confess with my mouth, 'Jesus is Lord', and believe in my heart that God raised him from the dead, I will be saved. For it is with my heart that I believe and am justified, and it is with my mouth that I confess and am saved. The Word of God is living and active. Sharper than any double-edged sword, it penetrates even to dividing my soul and spirit, my joints and marrow; it judges the thoughts and attitudes of my heart.

(Matt. 5:8; 11:29; 9:22; 13:15, 19; 15:18–19; Rom. 2:5; Luke 6:45; Matt. 22:37; 6:21; Acts 1:24; 13:22; 15:8; Luke 8:15; Rom. 10:8–10; Heb. 4:12)

33

A Sincere Heart

Because of God's mercy I do not lose heart. Though outwardly I am wasting away, yet inwardly I am being renewed day by day. I want the eyes of my heart to be enlightened in order that I may know the hope to which he has called me, the riches of his glorious inheritance in the saints.

It is God's purpose for me that I may be encouraged in my heart and united in love, so that I may have the full riches of complete understanding, in order that I may know the mystery of God, namely, Christ, in whom are hidden all the treasures of wisdom and knowledge. My heart is glad and so my tongue rejoices; my body also lives in hope!

God's command to me is to love from a pure heart and a good conscience and a sincere faith. I flee the evil desires of youth, and pursue righteousness, faith, love and peace, along with those who call on the Lord out of a pure heart. I am to see to it that I do not have a sinful, unbelieving heart that turns away from the living God.

I draw near to God with a sincere heart in full assurance of faith, having my heart sprinkled to cleanse me from a guilty conscience and having my body washed with pure water. I consider Jesus who endured such opposition from sinful men, so that I will not grow weary and lose heart.

I should not forget the word of encouragement that addresses me as a son: 'My son, do not make light of the Lord's discipline, and do not lose heart when he rebukes you.' I purify myself by obeying the truth so that I have sincere love for my brothers, loving others deeply, from the heart. Because I believe in the Son of God I have this testimony in my heart. I am not to set my heart on what I will eat or drink; I do not worry about such things.

If I say to this mountain (this problem in my life), 'Go, throw yourself into the sea', and do not doubt in my heart but believe that what I say will happen, it will be done for me. Jesus promises this.

(2 Cor. 4:16; Eph. 1:18; Col. 2:2; Acts 2:26; 1 Tim. 1:5; 2 Tim. 2:22; Heb. 3:12; 10:22; 12:3, 5; 1 Pet. 1:22; 1 John 5:10; Luke 12:29; Mark 11:23)

34

Light

In Jesus was life, and that life was the light of men. I have seen a great light; on me a light has dawned. Jesus is the light of the world. As I follow him I will never walk in darkness, but will have the light of life.

I put my trust in the light while I have it, so that I may become a son of light. I put aside the deeds of darkness and put on the armour of light. Because I live by the truth I come into the light, so that it may be seen plainly that what I have done has been done through God.

God, who said, 'Let light shine out of darkness', made his light shine in my heart to give me the light of the knowledge of the glory of God in the face of Christ. I was once darkness, but now I am light in the Lord. So I live as a child of light (for the fruit of the light consists in all goodness, righteousness and truth). The Father has qualified me to share in the inheritance of the saints in the kingdom of light.

I am a son of the light and a son of the day. I do not belong to the night or to the darkness. God has called me out of darkness into his wonderful light. If I walk in the light, as he is in the light, I have fellowship with others, and the blood of Jesus, his Son, purifies me from all sin.

The eye is the lamp of the body. If my eyes are good, my whole body will be full of light. But if my eyes are bad, my whole body will be full of darkness. I am to be light for the world. My light is to shine before men, that they may see my good deeds and praise my Father in heaven. If I love my brother I live in the light, and there is nothing in me to make him stumble.

(John 1:4; Matt. 4:16; John 8:12; 12:36; Rom. 13:12; John 3:21; 2 Cor. 4:6; Eph. 5:8; Col. 1:12; 1 Thess. 5:5; 1 Pet. 2:9; 1 John 1:7; Matt. 6:22–3; 5:14, 16; 1 John 2:10)

35

My Shepherd

Jesus is the Good Shepherd. The Good Shepherd lays down his life for the sheep. The hired hand is not the shepherd who owns the sheep. So when he sees the wolf coming, he abandons the sheep and runs away. Then the wolf attacks the flock and scatters it.

Jesus is the Good Shepherd; he knows me as one of his sheep and I know him. The Lord is my Shepherd, I shall not be in want. The Lord is my Shepherd and he carries me for ever.

For I was like a sheep going astray, but now I have returned to the Shepherd and overseer of my soul. When the Chief Shepherd appears, I will receive the crown of glory that will never fade away.

For the Lamb at the centre of the throne will be my Shepherd; he will lead me to springs of living water. And God will wipe away every tear from my eyes.

(John 10:11–12, 14; Ps. 23:1; 28:9; 1 Pet. 2:25; 5:4; Rev. 7:17)

36

Doing God's Will

For the grace of God that brings salvation has appeared to me. It teaches me to say no to ungodliness and worldly passions, and to live a self-controlled, upright and godly life in this present age, while I wait for the blessed hope – the glorious appearing of my great God and Saviour, Jesus Christ, who gave himself for me to redeem me from all wickedness, and to purify me for himself, to be his very own, eager to do what is good. But if I do sin, I have one who speaks to the Father in my defence, Jesus Christ, the Righteous One. He is the atoning sacrifice for my sins, and not only for mine but also for the sins of the whole world.

Because he himself suffered when he was tempted, he is able to help me when I am tempted. Therefore, since I have a great high priest who has gone through the heavens, Jesus the Son of God, I hold firmly to the faith I profess. For I do not have a high priest who is unable to sympathise with my weaknesses, but I have one who has been tempted in every way, just as I am – yet was without sin. I therefore approach the throne of grace with confidence, so that I may receive mercy and find grace to help me in my time of need.

I cast all my anxiety on him because he cares for me. If I confess my sins he is faithful and just to forgive me my sins and purify me from all unrighteousness.

Since I have been raised with Christ, I set my heart on things above, where Christ is seated at the right hand of God. I set my mind on things above, not on earthly things. I died to sin; how can I live in it any longer?

And whatever I do, whether in word or deed, I do it all in the name of the Lord Jesus, giving thanks to God the Father through him. Whatever I do, I work at it with all my heart, as working for the Lord, not for men, since I know that I will receive an inheritance from the Lord as a reward. It is the Lord Christ I am serving.

If I obey his word, God's love is truly made complete in me. The

God of peace, who through the blood of the eternal covenant brought back from the dead my Lord Jesus, that great Shepherd of the sheep, equips me with everything for doing his will. And he works in me what is pleasing to him, through Jesus Christ, to whom be glory for ever and ever. Amen.

(Titus 2:11–14; 1 John 2:1–2; Heb. 2:18; 4:14–16; 1 Pet. 5:7; 1 John 1:9; Col. 3:1–2, 17, 23–4; 1 John 2:5; Heb. 13:20–1)

37

Remaining in his Love

———◦———

How great is the love the Father has lavished on me that I should be called a child of God! And that is what I am! Now I am God's child, and what I will be has not yet been made known. But I know that when he appears I shall be like him, for I shall see him as he is. Because I have this hope I purify myself, just as he is pure.

As the Father has loved Jesus, so Jesus has loved me. Now I remain in his love. If I obey his commands I will remain in his love, just as he obeyed his Father's commands and remained in his love. Because of these truths his joy is in me and my joy is made complete. If I remain in Jesus and his words remain in me, I can ask whatever I wish and it will be given to me. This is to the Father's glory, that I bear much fruit, showing myself to be his disciple.

The anointing I received from him remains in me, and I do not need anyone to teach me. But as this anointing teaches me about all things, and as that anointing is real, not counterfeit, just as it has taught me, I remain in him. I continue in him, so that when he appears I may be confident and unashamed before him at his coming.

I do not let anyone lead me astray. If I do what is right I am righteous, just as he is righteous. He who does what is sinful is of the devil, because the devil has been sinning from the beginning. The reason the Son of God appeared was to destroy the devil's works. Because I am born of God I will not continue to sin, because God's seed remains in me; I cannot go on sinning, because I have been born of God.

By obeying his commands I live in him, and he in me. And this is how I know he lives in me: I know it by the Spirit he gave me. Because I love Jesus I will obey his teaching. The Father will love me and he and Jesus come to me and make their home with me. If I continue in the teaching of Jesus, I have both the Father and the Son.

I pray that my love may abound more and more in knowledge and depth of insight so that I may be able to discern what is best, and may be pure and blameless until the day of Christ, filled with the fruit of righteousness that comes through Jesus Christ to the glory and praise of God. Just as I received Christ Jesus as Lord, I continue to live in him, rooted and built up in him, strengthened in the faith as I was taught, and overflowing with thankfulness.

(1 John 3:1–3; John 15:9–11, 7–8; 1 John 2:27–8; 3:7–9, 24; John 14:23; 2 John 9; Phil. 1:9–11; Col. 2:6–7)

38

Overcoming

Because I am born of God I have overcome the world. This is the victory that has overcome the world, even my faith. Who is it that overcomes the world? I do, because I believe that Jesus is the Son of God. Everything is possible for me because I believe. I can do everything through him who gives me strength.

Because I have faith in Jesus, I will do what he has been doing. I will do even greater things than these because he has returned to the Father. If I say to this mountain (this problem in my life), 'Go, throw yourself into the sea', and do not doubt in my heart but believe that what I say will happen, it will be done for me. Therefore whatever I ask for in prayer, I am to believe that I have received it and it will be mine.

He who did not spare his own Son but gave him up for me, will he not also, along with him, graciously give me all things? My God will meet all my needs according to his glorious riches in Christ Jesus.

If I give it will be given to me. Good measure, pressed down, shaken together and running over, will be poured into my lap. For with the measure I use it will be measured to me.

If I agree with anyone else on earth about anything I ask for, it will be done for me by my Father in heaven. For no matter how many promises God has made, they are 'Yes' in Christ. And so through him the 'Amen' is spoken by me to the glory of God.

(1 John 5:4–5; Mark 9:23; Phil. 4:13; John 14:12; Mark 11:23–4; Rom. 8:32; Phil. 4:19; Luke 6:38; Matt. 18:19; 2 Cor. 1:20)

39

My Hope in God

I do not put my hope in wealth, which is so uncertain, but I put my hope in God, who richly provides me with everything for my enjoyment. Having been justified by his grace, I have become an heir having the hope of eternal life. I put on hope of salvation as a helmet.

I am to show diligence to the very end, in order to make my hope sure. I hold unswervingly to the hope I profess, for he who promised is faithful. Now faith is being sure of what I hope for and certain of what I do not see.

I prepare my mind for action; I am to be self-controlled; I set my hope fully on the grace to be given to me when Jesus Christ is revealed. Through Jesus I believe in God, who raised him from the dead and glorified him, and so my faith and hope are in God. Because I have this hope in him I purify myself, just as he is pure.

On him I have set my hope that he will continue to deliver me. Praise be to the God and Father of our Lord Jesus Christ! In his great mercy he has given me new birth into a living hope through the resurrection of Jesus Christ from the dead. I rejoice in the hope of the glory of God.

For everything that was written in the past was written to teach me, so that through endurance and the encouragement of the Scriptures I might have hope. Hope does not disappoint me, because God has poured out his love into my heart by the Holy Spirit, whom he has given me. The God of hope fills me with all joy and peace as I trust in him, so that I may overflow with hope by the power of the Holy Spirit.

If I hope for what I do not yet have, I wait for it patiently. I am joyful in hope, patient in affliction, faithful in prayer.

If only for this life I have hope in Christ, I am to be pitied more than all men. I pray that the eyes of my heart may be enlightened in order that I may know the hope to which he has called me, the riches of his glorious inheritance in the saints.

But by faith I eagerly await through the Spirit the righteousness for which I hope. Faith and love spring from the hope that is stored up for me in heaven. I am to continue in my faith, established and firm, not moved from the hope held out in the gospel. My work is to be produced by faith, my labour prompted by love, and my endurance inspired by hope in my Lord Jesus Christ.

I have put my hope in the living God, who is the Saviour of all men, and especially of those who believe.

God has chosen to make known to me the glorious riches of this mystery, which is Christ in me, the hope of glory. Since I have such a hope, I am very bold.

(1 Tim. 6:17; Titus 3:7; 1 Thess. 5:8; Heb. 6:18; 10:23; 11:1; 1 Pet. 1:13, 21; 1 John 3:3; 2 Cor. 1:10; 1 Pet. 1:3; Rom. 5:2; 15:4; 5:5; 15:13; 8:25; 12:12; 1 Cor. 15:19; Gal. 5:5; Col. 1:5, 23; 1 Thess. 1:3; 1 Tim. 4:10; Col. 1:27; 2 Cor. 3:12)

40

Victory

I submit myself, then, to God. I resist the devil and he flees from me. I come near to God and he comes near to me. It is for freedom Christ has set me free. I stand firm, then, and do not let myself be burdened again by a yoke of slavery. Therefore I stand firm. I let nothing move me. I always give myself fully to the work of the Lord, because I know that my labour in the Lord is not in vain.

Now it is God who makes me stand firm in Christ. He anointed me, set his seal of ownership on me and put his Spirit in my heart as a deposit, guaranteeing what is to come. I am to be strong in the grace that is in Christ Jesus. I am to be strong in the Lord and in his mighty power.

Jesus gives me his word, so that in him I may have peace. In this world I will have trouble. But I take heart! He has overcome the world! No, in all these things I am more than a conqueror through him who loved me. The sting of death is sin, and the power of sin is the law. But thanks be to God! He gives me the victory through my Lord Jesus Christ. Thanks be to God, who always leads me in triumphal procession in Christ, and through me spreads everywhere the fragrance of the knowledge of him.

Because I have received God's abundant grace and am freely put right with him, I will rule in life through Christ. I have been given authority to trample on snakes and scorpions, and to overcome all the power of the enemy; nothing will harm me. However, I do not rejoice that the spirits submit to me, but I rejoice that my name is written in heaven.

To be sure, he was crucified in weakness, yet he lives by God's power. Likewise I am weak in him, yet by God's power I will live with him to serve others. I will be changed – in a flash, in the twinkling of an eye, at the last trumpet. For the trumpet will sound, the dead will be raised imperishable and I will be changed.

(Jas. 4:7–8; Gal. 5:1; 1 Cor. 15:58; 2 Cor. 1:21–2; 2 Tim. 2:1; Eph. 6:10; John 16:33; Rom. 8:37; 1 Cor. 15:56–7; 2 Cor. 2:14; Rom. 5:17; Luke 10:18–20; 2 Cor. 13:4; 1 Cor. 15:51–2)

41

Made Holy

This is love, not that I loved God but that he loved me and sent his Son as an atoning sacrifice for my sins. For Christ died for sins once for all, the righteous for the unrighteous to bring me to God. He was put to death in the body but made alive by the Spirit. When I turned to the Lord the veil separating me from God was taken away. Now the Lord is the Spirit, and where the Spirit of the Lord is there is freedom.

He too shared in my humanity, so that by his death he might destroy him who holds the power of death – that is, the devil – and free me from being held in slavery by the fear of death. He entered heaven itself, now to appear for me in God's presence. He is able to save me completely because I have come to God through him, and he always lives to intercede for me. Such a high priest meets my need, one who is holy, blameless, pure, set apart from sinners, exalted above the heavens.

Jesus suffered to make me holy through his own blood. By his will I have been made holy through the sacrifice of the body of Jesus Christ once for all. By one sacrifice he has made perfect for ever those who are being made holy, *including me!* I was washed, I was sanctified, I was justified in the name of the Lord Jesus Christ and by the Spirit of my God.

For God has brought me into union with Christ Jesus, and God has made Christ to be my wisdom. By him I am put right with God – I become one of God's holy people and am set free. I am sanctified in Christ Jesus and called to be holy, together with all those everywhere who call on the name of the Lord Jesus Christ, their Lord and mine.

In him I am being built together with others to become a dwelling in which God lives by his Spirit. In Christ I form one body with the other members, and I belong to all the other members.

(1 John 4:10; 1 Pet. 3:18; 2 Cor. 3:16–17; Heb. 2:14–15; 9:24; 7:25–6; 13:12; 10:10, 14; 1 Cor. 6:11; 1:30, 2; Eph. 2:21–2; Rom. 12:4–5)

42

His Joy within Me

Jesus speaks through his Word that his joy may be in me and that my joy may be complete. Jesus was full of joy through the Holy Spirit, and said, 'I praise you, Father, Lord of heaven and earth, because you have hidden these things from the wise and learned, and revealed them to little children. Yes, Father, for this was your good pleasure.'

Jesus speaks these things to me through his Word, so that I may have the full measure of his joy within me. I am filled with joy and with the Holy Spirit. God has made known to me the path of life; he fills me with joy in his presence. He provides for me and fills my heart with joy.

For the kingdom of God is not a matter of eating and drinking, but of righteousness, peace and joy in the Holy Spirit. The God of hope fills me with all joy and peace as I trust in him, so that I may overflow with hope by the power of the Holy Spirit. No one can take away my joy! I want others to share my joy.

I am greatly encouraged; in all my troubles my joy knows no bounds. Even in the most severe trials, my overflowing joy is to well up in rich generosity. I consider it pure joy whenever I face trials of many kinds, because I know the testing of my faith produces perseverance.

I am to rejoice and leap for joy when persecuted, because great is my reward in heaven. Joy is part of the fruit of the Spirit in my life.

My joy in Christ Jesus is to overflow. I am always to pray with joy. If I ask I will receive, and my joy will be complete. Jesus promises this.

(John 15:11; Luke 10:21; John 17:13; Acts 13:52; 2:28; 14:17; Rom. 14:17; 15:13; John 16:22; 2 Cor. 2:3; 7:4; 8:2; Jas. 1:2; Luke 2:10; Gal. 5:22; Phil. 1:26; 1:4; John 16:24)

43

Great Joy

I fix my eyes on Jesus, the author and perfecter of my faith, who for the joy set before him endured the cross, scorning its shame, and sat down at the right hand of the throne of God. Jesus loved righteousness and hated wickedness; therefore God, his God, has set him above his companions by anointing him with the oil of joy.

Though I have not seen him, I love him; and even though I do not see him now, I believe in him and am filled with an inexpressible and glorious joy. The Lord is able to keep me from falling and to present me before his glorious presence without fault and with great joy!

I greatly rejoice, though now for a little while I may have had to suffer grief in all kinds of trials. These have come so that my faith – of greater worth than gold, which perishes even though refined by fire – may be proved genuine and may result in praise, glory and honour when Jesus Christ is revealed. And after I have suffered a little while, the God of all grace – who imparts all blessing and favour – who has called me to his own eternal glory in Christ Jesus, will himself complete and make me what I ought to be, establish and ground me securely, and strengthen and settle me. To him be the dominion – power, authority, rule – for ever and ever. Amen – so be it.

I welcome the message of the gospel with the joy given to me by the Holy Spirit.

(Heb. 12:2; 1:9; 1 Pet. 1:8; Jude v. 24; 1 Pet. 1:6–7; 5:10–11 (Amplified Version); 1 Thess. 1:6)

44

Jesus's Glory

Jesus did not seek glory for himself; if that was true of him, it certainly needs to be true of me. Jesus said that if he glorified himself, his glory would mean nothing. His Father was the one who glorified him. If I glorify myself, my glory means nothing therefore. Jesus brought the Father glory on earth by completing the work he gave him to do. I will likewise bring him glory by completing what he gives me to do.

Jesus says, if I believe, I will see the glory of God. The Holy Spirit brings glory to Jesus by taking from what is his and making it known to me. I glorify the Father by bearing much fruit, showing myself to be Jesus's disciple.

Jesus gives to his disciples the glory that the Father gave him, that they may be one as the Father and Son are one. I am a disciple to whom he gives his glory. Jesus wants me to be with him where he now is, and to see his glory, the glory the Father has given him because he loved him before the creation of the world.

When the Son of Man comes in his Father's glory with his angels, he will reward each person according to what he has done, *including me!* When the Son of Man comes in his glory, and all the angels with him, he will sit on his throne in heavenly glory. If anyone is ashamed of Jesus and his words in this adulterous and sinful generation, the Son of Man will be ashamed of him when he comes in his Father's glory with the holy angels.

(John 8:50, 54; 17:4; 11:40; 16:14; 15:8; 17:22, 24; Matt. 16:27; 25:31; Mark 8:38)

45

Reflecting the Lord's Glory

To those who by persistence in doing good seek glory, honour and immortality, the Lord will give eternal life. I rejoice in the hope of the glory of God.

I was buried with Christ through baptism into death in order that, just as he was raised from the dead through the glory of the Father, I too may live a new life. Now if I am a child of God, then I am an heir – an heir of God and a co-heir with Christ, if indeed I share in his sufferings in order that I may also share in his glory. I consider that my present sufferings are not worth comparing with the glory that will be revealed in me.

With an unveiled face I reflect the Lord's glory, and am being transformed into his likeness with ever-increasing glory, which comes from the Lord, who is the Spirit. God, who said, 'Let light shine out of darkness', made his light shine in my heart to give me the light of the knowledge of the glory of God in the face of Christ.

I confess that Jesus Christ is Lord, to the glory of God the Father. Because I worship by the Spirit of God, I glory in Christ Jesus, and put no confidence in the flesh.

God has chosen to make known to me the glorious riches of this mystery, which is Christ in me, the hope of glory. When Christ, who is my life, appears, then I also will appear with him in glory.

My light and momentary troubles are achieving for me an eternal glory that far outweighs them all.

God called me to share in the gospel, that I might share in the glory of my Lord Jesus Christ. I am urged to live a life worthy of God, who calls me into his kingdom and glory. The Lord will rescue me from every evil attack and will bring me safely to his heavenly kingdom. To him be glory for ever and ever. Amen.

(Rom. 2:7; 6:4; 8:17; 2 Cor. 3:18; 4:6; Phil. 2:11; 3:3; Col. 1:27; 3:4; 2 Cor. 4:17; 2 Thess. 2:14; 1 Thess. 2:12; 2 Tim. 4:18)

46

The Spirit of Glory

The Son is the radiance of God's glory and the exact representation of his being, sustaining all things by his powerful word. After he had provided purification for sins, he sat down at the right hand of the Majesty in heaven. Jesus was made a little lower than the angels; he is now crowned with glory and honour. He is now crowned with glory and honour because he suffered death, so that by the grace of God he might taste death for everyone, ***including me!***

In bringing many sons to glory, it was fitting that God, for whom and through whom everything exists, should make the author of their salvation perfect through suffering. This is what it cost him to bring me to glory.

Trials come so that my faith – of greater worth than gold, which perishes even though refined by fire – may be proved genuine and may result in praise, glory and honour when Jesus Christ is revealed. I rejoice that I participate in the sufferings of Christ, so that I may be overjoyed when his glory is revealed. If I am insulted because of the name of Christ, I am blessed, for the Spirit of glory and of God rests on me.

The God of all grace has called me to his eternal glory in Christ. Even if I suffer for a little while, he will himself restore me and make me strong, firm and steadfast. His divine power has given me everything I need for life and godliness through my knowledge of him who called me by his own glory and goodness. When the Chief Shepherd appears, I will receive the crown of glory that will never fade away.

(Heb. 1:3; 2:7, 9, 10; 1 Pet. 1:7; 4:13, 14; 5:10; 2 Pet. 1:3; 1 Pet. 5:4)

47

Jesus's Authority in Me

All authority in heaven and on earth has been given to Jesus, and I live in him! People were amazed at Jesus's teaching, because his message had authority. He calls me to proclaim that same message. The people were amazed and realised that it was part of Jesus's teaching for him to give orders with authority and power to evil spirits; and they come out!

Jesus commended the centurion for his faith for he understood authority. He was a man under authority and so could exercise authority over those placed under him. I am under the authority of Jesus and can exercise authority over everything he places under me.

Jesus demonstrated his authority to forgive sins by commanding the paralysed man to get up, take his mat and go home. He gives me authority to forgive sins in his name.

Jesus has given me authority to trample on snakes and scorpions and to overcome all the power of the enemy; nothing will harm me. As his disciple Jesus has given me authority to drive out evil spirits and to heal every disease and sickness. Jesus has authority to judge because he is the Son of Man. His word says I am able to judge all things.

Jesus is far above all rule and authority, power and dominion, and every title that can be given, not only in the present age but also in the one to come.

Jesus was granted authority over all people, *including me!*

And I have been given fullness in Christ, who is the head over every power and authority.

(Matt. 28:18; Luke 4:32, 36; 7:8; 5:24; 10:19; Matt. 10:1; John 5:27; Eph. 1:21; John 17:2; Col. 2:10)

48

Submission to Authority

I am to encourage and rebuke with all authority. I am not to let anyone despise me. The Lord does not want me to be harsh in my use of authority – the authority the Lord gave me for building others up, not for tearing them down.

The law has authority over a man only as long as he lives. Because I have died to the religious law, it no longer has any authority over me.

I am to recognise the authority which God has established. The authorities that exist have been established by God. Consequently, I am not to rebel against the authority for that is rebelling against what God has instituted, and those who do so will bring judgment on themselves. Rulers hold no terror for me if I do right. I want to be free from fear of the one in authority. Then I do what is right and I will be commended.

I am to submit myself for the Lord's sake to every authority instituted among men.

The Lord wants me to pray for those in authority, that we may live peaceful and quiet lives in all godliness and holiness.

I am to obey my leaders and submit to their authority. They keep watch over me as men who must give an account. I am to obey them so that their work will be a joy, not a burden, for that would be of no advantage to me.

To him who overcomes and does his will to the end, Jesus will give authority over the nations. I will overcome and persevere in doing his work.

To the only God our Saviour be glory, majesty, power and authority, through Jesus Christ our Lord, before all ages, now and for evermore! Amen.

(Titus 2:15; 2 Cor. 13:10; Rom. 7:1; 13:1–3; 1 Pet. 2:13; 1 Tim. 2:2; Heb. 13:17; Rev. 2:26; Jude 1:25)

PART 3

Jesus Speaks Directly to You Through Matthew's Gospel: Collections of Related Sayings

Introduction

In this Part I have taken verses from Matthew's Gospel as representation of the material given in the synoptic gospels (Matthew, Mark and Luke). These sections are direct quotes from the biblical text: Jesus is talking to you personally, as for example with the sections from the Sermon on the Mount.

In other sections I have collected verses relating to a particular subject. There is great value in doing this yourself, for in this way you discover what Jesus himself says about a particular subject. And his Word is far superior to the views of any man or woman!

49

The Beatitudes

Now when he saw the crowds, he went up on a mountainside and sat down. His disciples came to him, and he began to teach them, saying:

Blessed are the poor in spirit, for theirs is the kingdom of heaven.
Blessed are those who mourn, for they will be comforted.
Blessed are the meek, for they will inherit the earth.
Blessed are those who hunger and thirst for righteousness, for they will be filled.
Blessed are the merciful, for they will be shown mercy.
Blessed are the pure in heart, for they will see God.
Blessed are the peacemakers, for they will be called sons of God.
Blessed are those who are persecuted because of righteousness, for theirs is the kingdom of heaven.
Blessed are you when people insult you, persecute you and falsely say all kinds of evil against you because of me.
Rejoice and be glad, because great is your reward in heaven, for in the same way they persecuted the prophets who were before you. (Matt. 5:1–12)

50

Forgive

You have heard that it was said to the people long ago, 'Do not murder, and anyone who murders will be subject to judgment.' But I tell you that if you are angry with your brother (without cause) you will be subject to judgment. Therefore, if you are offering your gift at the altar and there remember that your brother has something against you, leave your gift there in front of the altar. First go and be reconciled to your brother; then come and offer your gift. (Matt. 5:17–24)

You have heard that it was said, 'An eye for an eye, and a tooth for a tooth.' But I tell you, do not resist an evil person. If someone strikes you on the right cheek, turn to him the other also. And if someone wants to sue you and take your tunic, let him have your cloak as well. If someone forces you to go one mile, go with him two miles. Give to the one who asks you, and do not turn away from the one who wants to borrow from you. (Matt. 5:38–42)

For if you forgive men when they sin against you, your heavenly Father will also forgive you. But if you do not forgive men their sins, your Father will not forgive your sins. (Matt. 6:14–15)

Do not judge, or you too will be judged. For in the same way as you judge others, you will be judged, and with the measure you use, it will be measured to you. Why do you look at the speck of sawdust in your brother's eye and pay no attention to the plank in your own eye? How can you say to your brother 'Let me take the speck out of your eye,' when all the time there is a plank in your own eye? You hypocrite, first take the plank out of your own eye, and then you will see clearly to remove the speck from your brother's eye. (Matt. 7:1–5)

If your brother sins against you, go and show him his fault, just between the two of you. If he listens to you, you have won your brother over. But if he will not listen, take one or two others along, so that every matter may be established by the testimony of two or three witnesses. If he refuses to listen to them, tell it to the church; and if he refuses to listen even to the church, treat him as you would an outcast. (Matt. 18:15–17)

51

Everything will be Added to You

Do not store up for yourself treasures on earth, where moth and rust destroy, and where thieves break in and steal. But store up for yourself treasures in heaven, where moth and rust do not destroy, and where thieves do not break in and steal. For where your treasure is, there your heart will be also. (Matt. 6:19–21)

No one can serve two masters. Either he will hate the one and love the other, or he will be devoted to the one and despise the other. You cannot serve both God and money. (Matt. 6:24)

Therefore, I tell you, do not worry about your life, what you will eat or drink; or about your body, what you will wear. Is not life more important than food, and the body more important than clothes? Look at the birds of the air; they do not sow or reap or store away in barns, and yet your heavenly Father feeds them. Are you not much more valuable than they? (Matt. 6:25–6)

Who of you by worrying can add a single hour to his life? And why do you worry about clothes? See how the lilies of the field grow. They do not labour or spin. Yet I tell you that not even Solomon in all his splendour was dressed like one of these. If that is how God clothes the grass of the field, which is here today and tomorrow is thrown into the fire, will he not much more clothe you, O you of little faith? (Matt. 6:27–30)

So do not worry, saying, 'What shall I eat?' or 'What shall I drink?' or 'What shall I wear?' For the pagans run after all these things, and your heavenly Father knows that you need them. But seek first his kingdom and his righteousness, and all these things will be given to you as well. Therefore do not worry about tomorrow, for tomorrow will worry about itself. Each day has enough trouble of its own. (Matt. 6:30–4)

52
Ask

Ask and it will be given to you; seek and you will find; knock and the door will be opened to you. For everyone who asks receives; he who seeks finds; and to him who knocks, the door will be opened. (Matt. 7:7)

Which of you, if his son asks for bread, will give him a stone? Or if he asks for a fish, will give him a snake? If you, then, though you are evil, know how to give good gifts to your children, how much more will your Father in heaven give good gifts to those who ask him! So in everything, do to others what you would have them do to you, for this sums up the Law and the Prophets. (Matt. 7:9–12)

I tell you the truth, if you have faith as small as a mustard seed, you can say to this mountain, 'Move from here to there' and it will move. Nothing will be impossible for you. (Matt. 17:20)

I tell you the truth, whatever you bind on earth will be bound in heaven, and whatever you loose on earth will be loosed in heaven. (Matt. 18:18)

Again, I tell you that if two of you on earth agree about anything you ask for, it will be done for you by my Father in heaven. For where two or three come together in my name, there am I with them. (Matt. 18:19–20)

With God all things are possible. (Matt. 19:26)

I tell you the truth, if you have faith and do not doubt, not only can you do what was done to the fig tree, but also you can say to this mountain, 'Go, throw yourself into the sea', and it will be done. If you believe, you will receive whatever you ask for in prayer. (Matt. 21:21–2)

Because you have you will be given more, and you will have an abundance. Whoever does not have, even what he has will be taken from him. (Matt. 25:29)

53

The Narrow Gate

Enter through the narrow gate. For wide is the gate and broad is the road that leads to destruction, and many enter through it. But small is the gate and narrow the road that leads to life, and only a few find it. (Matt. 8:13–14)

Watch out for false prophets. They come to you in sheep's clothing, but inwardly they are ferocious wolves. By their fruit you will recognise them. Do people pick grapes from thorn bushes, or figs from thistles? Likewise every good tree bears good fruit, but a bad tree bears bad fruit. A good tree cannot bear bad fruit, and a bad tree cannot bear good fruit. Every tree that does not bear good fruit is cut down and thrown into the fire. Thus, by their fruit you will recognise them. (Matt. 8:15–20)

Not everyone who says to me, 'Lord, Lord' will enter the kingdom of heaven, but only he who does the will of my Father who is in heaven. Many will say to me on that day, 'Lord, Lord, did we not prophesy in your name, and in your name drive out demons and perform many miracles?' Then I will tell them plainly, 'I never knew you. Away from me, you evildoers!' (Matt. 8:21–3)

Therefore, if you hear these words of mine and put them into practice you are like a wise man who built his house on the rock. The rain came down, the streams rose, and the winds blew and beat against that house; yet it did not fall, because it had its foundation on the rock. But if you hear these words of mine and do not put them into practice you are like a foolish man who built his house on sand. The rain came down, the streams rose, and the winds blew and beat against that house, and it fell with a great crash. (Matt. 8:24–7)

54

Be Healed

'I am willing, be clean!' 'Go! It will be done just as you believed it would.' (Matt. 8:3, 13)

When evening came, many who were possessed by demons were brought to him, and he drove out the spirits with a word and healed all the sick. This was to fulfil what was spoken through the prophet Isaiah: 'I took up your infirmities and carried your diseases.' (Matt. 8:16–17)

Jesus said, 'It is not the healthy who need a doctor, but the sick.' (Matt. 9:12)

'Take heart, daughter, your faith has healed you.' (Matt. 9:22)

'Do you believe that I am able to do this?' 'According to your faith will it be done to you.' (Matt. 9:28–9)

Jesus went through all the towns and villages, teaching in their synagogues, preaching the good news of the kingdom and healing every disease and sickness. When he saw the crowds, he had compassion on them, because they were harassed and helpless, like sheep without a shepherd. Then he said to his disciples, 'The harvest is plentiful but the workers are few. Ask the Lord of the harvest, therefore, to send out workers into his harvest field.' (Matt. 9:35–8)

I give you authority to drive out evil spirits and to heal every disease and sickness. As you go, preach this message: 'The kingdom of heaven is near.' Heal the sick, raise the dead, cleanse those who have leprosy, drive out demons. Freely you have received, freely give. (Matt. 10:1, 7–8)

The blind receive sight, the lame walk, those who have leprosy are cured, the deaf hear, the dead are raised, and the good news is preached to the poor. (Matt. 11:5)

'Woman, you have great faith! Your request is granted.' And her daughter was healed from that very hour. (Matt. 15:28)

Great crowds came to him, bringing the lame, the blind, the

crippled, the mute and many others, and laid them at his feet; and he healed them. (Matt. 15:30)

Jesus had compassion on them and touched their eyes. Immediately they received their sight and followed him. (Matt. 20:34)

And he did not do many miracles there because of their lack of faith. (Matt. 13:58)

55

The Kingdom of Heaven

The knowledge of the secrets of the kingdom of heaven has been given to you, but not to them. Whoever has will be given more, and he will have an abundance. Whoever does not have, even what he has will be taken from him. (Matt. 13:11–12)

I tell you the truth, unless you change and become like a little child, you will never enter the kingdom of heaven. Therefore, if you humble yourself like this child you are great in the kingdom of heaven. And if you welcome a little child like this in my name you welcome me. But if you cause one of these little ones who believe in me to sin, it would be better for you to have a large millstone hung around your neck and to be drowned in the depths of the sea. (Matt. 18:3–6)

What do you think? There was a man who had two sons. He went to the first and said, 'Son, go and work today in the vineyard.' 'I will not,' he answered, but later he changed his mind and went. Then the father went to the other son and said the same thing. He answered, 'I will, sir,' but he did not go. Which of the two did what his father wanted? The first, they answered. (Matt. 21:28–31)

Heaven and earth will pass away, but my words will never pass away. No one knows about that day or hour, not even the angels in heaven, nor the Son, but only the Father. (Matt. 24:35–6)

56

Discipleship

If you love your father or mother more than me you are not worthy of me; if you love your son or daughter more than me you are not worthy of me; and if you do not take your cross and follow me you are not worthy of me. If you find your life you will lose it, and if you lose your life for my sake you will find it. (Matt. 10:37–9)

For whoever does the will of my Father in heaven is my brother and sister and mother. (Matt. 12:50)

If you would come after me, you must deny yourself and take up your cross and follow me. For if you want to save your life you will lose it, but if you lose your life for me you will find it. What good will it be for you if you gain the whole world, yet forfeit your soul? Or what can you give in exchange for your soul? For the Son of Man is going to come in his Father's glory with his angels, and then he will reward you according to what you have done. (Matt. 16:24–7)

And everyone who has left houses or brothers or sisters or father or mother (or wife) or children or fields for my sake will receive a hundred times as much and will inherit eternal life. But many who are first will be last, and many who are last will be first. (Matt. 19:29–30)

Come to me, whenever you are weary and burdened, and I will give you rest. Take my yoke upon you and learn from me, for I am gentle and humble in heart, and you will find rest for your soul. For my yoke is easy and my burden is light. (Matt. 11:28–30)

PART 4

Collections of Sayings About God as Your Father: Applying These Truths to Your Life

Introduction

In this Part we have sections containing New Testament references to God as your Father. Many of the verses used have been written as statements which apply the truth to my life, so that I can see clearly what I am to believe about God as my Father, how I am to relate to him as Father and what it means to put his Word into practice in my life. This is a very simple way of writing your own interpretation of Scripture, but staying very close to the biblical text in the process. You are interpreting the truth by relating it to your own life and experience.

57

The Sermon on the Mount

My light is to shine before men, that they may see my good deeds and praise my Father in heaven. (Matt. 5:16)

I am to love my enemies and pray for those who persecute me that I may be a son of my Father in heaven. (Matt. 5:44–5)

Jesus calls me to be perfect, to be whole and complete in him, as my heavenly Father is perfect. (Matt. 5:48)

I must be careful not to do my 'acts of righteousness' before men, to be seen by them. If I do, I will have no reward from my Father in heaven. (Matt. 6:1)

I am to ensure that my giving is done in secret. Then my Father, who sees what is done in secret, will reward me. (Matt. 6:4)

When I pray, I am to go into my room, close the door and pray to my Father, who is unseen. Then my Father, who sees what is done in secret, will reward me. (Matt. 6:6)

My Father knows what I need before I ask him. (Matt. 6:8)

If I forgive men when they sin against me, my heavenly Father will also forgive me. But if I do not forgive men their sins, my Father will not forgive my sins. (Matt. 6:14)

I am much more valuable than the birds. So if my heavenly Father feeds them, he will certainly supply my needs. (Matt. 6:26)

I know how to give good gifts to my children; how much more does my Father in heaven give good gifts to me when I ask him! (Matt. 7:11)

Saying 'Lord, Lord' will not get me into the kingdom of heaven; I need to do the will of my Father who is in heaven. (Matt. 7:21)

58

Wonderful Truths

When put to the test I do not need to worry about what to say, for it will not be me speaking, but the Spirit of my Father speaking through me. (Matt. 10:20)

Because I acknowledge Jesus before men, he will also acknowledge me before his Father in heaven. Whoever disowns him before men, he will disown before his Father in heaven. (Matt. 10:32)

I am privileged and blessed that Jesus has chosen to reveal the Father to me. (Matt 11:27)

Doing the will of my Father in heaven numbers me among those Jesus regards as his brother and sister and mother. (Matt. 12:50)

As one made righteous by Jesus, I will shine like the sun in the kingdom of my Father. (Matt. 13:43)

If I agree with another about anything I ask for, and we are one in faith and love, it will be done for me by my Father in heaven. (Matt. 18:19)

I am to forgive my brother from my heart. (Matt. 18:35)

I have one Father and he is in heaven. (Matt. 23:9)

When I pray, if I hold anything against anyone, I am to forgive him, so that my Father in heaven may forgive me my sins. But if I do not forgive, neither will my Father who is in heaven forgive my sins. (Mark 11:25–6)

God is my 'Abba', my Father. Everything is possible for him. (Mark 14:36)

59

He Supplies my Needs

I am to be merciful, just as my Father is merciful. (Luke 6:36)

If I am ashamed of Jesus and his words, the Son of Man will be ashamed of me when he comes in glory and in the glory of the Father and of the holy angels. (Luke 9:26)

I know how to give good gifts to my children. How much more will my Father in heaven give the Holy Spirit to me when I ask him! (Luke 11:13)

My Father knows all that I need. (Luke 12:30)

There is no need for me to be afraid, for my Father has been pleased to give me his kingdom with all its riches and resources! (Luke 12:32)

God says to me: 'You are always with me, and everything I have is yours.' (Luke 15:31)

Jesus has conferred on me a kingdom, just as his Father conferred one on him! (Luke 22:29)

Jesus promises to send me what his Father has promised. By the Holy Spirit I have received power from on high. (Luke 24:29)

60

My Relationship with the Father and the Son

Jesus came from the Father, full of grace and truth. And he has revealed that grace and truth to us that I might know his glory. (John 1:14)

The Father loves the Son and has placed everything in his hands. (John 3:35)

As a true worshipper I worship the Father in spirit and truth. These are the kind of worshippers the Father seeks. (John 4:23)

Jesus said: 'My Father is always at his work to this very day, and I, too, am working.' I praise the Father that he is working in me! (John 5:17)

Jesus said that the Son could do nothing by himself; he could do only what he saw his Father doing, because whatever the Father does, the Son also does. I can do nothing myself. I need to do what Jesus did. (John 5:19)

For just as the Father raises the dead and gives them life, even so the Son gives life to whom he is pleased to give it. And he has been pleased to give that life to me. (John 5:21)

If I do not honour the Son, I do not honour the Father, who sent him. (John 5:23)

For as the Father has life in himself, so he has granted the Son to have life in himself. And I live in him who is the life. (John 5:26)

I do not work for food that spoils, but for food that endures to eternal life, which the Son of Man will give me. On him God the Father has placed his seal of approval, and because I am in him he has approved of me! (John 6:27)

My Father has given me the true bread from heaven. (John 6:32)

The Father has given me to Jesus. This is how I have come to him, and because I have come to Jesus, he will never drive me away. (John 6:37)

I could only have come to Jesus because the Father who sent him drew me to himself; and Jesus will raise me up at the last day. Because I listen to the Father and learn from him, I come to Jesus. (John 6:44–5)

I could not have come to Jesus unless the Father had enabled me. (John 6:65)

Because I know Jesus, I know his Father also. (John 8:19)

61

My Father Gives to Me

The Father has given me to Jesus as one of his sheep. No one can snatch me out of the Father's hand. (John 10:29)

I will be honoured by my heavenly Father if I serve Jesus. (John 12:26)

Because Jesus is the way and the truth and the life, I can only come to the Father through him. (John 14:6)

Jesus promises to do whatever I ask in his name, so that he may bring glory to the Father. (John 14:13)

Because I love Jesus, I am loved by his Father, and Jesus also loves me and shows himself to me. (John 14:21)

I show my love for Jesus by obeying his teaching. The Father therefore loves me, and both he and Jesus come to me and make their home with me. (John 14:23)

All that belongs to the Father belongs to Jesus. The Holy Spirit takes from what is his and makes it known to me. (John 16:15)

My heavenly Father will give me whatever I ask in the name of Jesus. (John 16:23)

The Father himself loves me because I have loved Jesus and have believed that he came from God. (John 16:27)

Jesus prayed that his Holy Father would protect me by the power of his name. (John 17:11)

62

My Loving Father

Grace and peace are mine from God the Father and from the Lord Jesus Christ. (Rom. 1:7)

I did not receive a spirit that makes me a slave again to fear, but I received the Spirit of sonship. And by him I cry, 'Abba, Father.' (Rom. 8:15)

There is but one God, the Father, from whom all things came and for whom I live; and there is but one Lord, Jesus Christ, through whom all things came and through whom I live. (1 Cor. 8:6)

He is the Father of compassion and the God of all comfort. (2 Cor. 1:3)

He is to be praised for ever. (2 Cor. 11:31)

Jesus gave himself for my sins to rescue me from the present evil age, according to the will of my God and Father. (Gal. 1:4)

I am a son of God. He has sent the Spirit of his Son into my heart, the Spirit who calls out, 'Abba, Father.' (Gal. 4:6)

He is the glorious Father, who gives me the Spirit of wisdom and revelation, so that I may know him better. (Eph. 1:17)

Through Jesus I have access to the Father by one Spirit. (Eph. 2:18)

There is one God and Father of all, who is over all and through all and in all. (Eph. 4:6)

I am always to give thanks to God the Father for everything, in the name of my Lord Jesus Christ. (Eph. 5:20)

63

I am Thankful to my Father

Love with faith is given to me from God the Father and the Lord Jesus Christ. (Eph. 6:23)

I confess that Jesus Christ is Lord, to the glory of God the Father. (Phil. 2:11)

The Father has qualified me to share in the inheritance of the saints in the kingdom of light. (Col. 1:12)

Whatever I do, whether in word or deed, I do it all in the name of the Lord Jesus, giving thanks to God the Father through him. (Col. 3:17)

As a member of the church I am in God the Father and the Lord Jesus Christ. (1 Thess. 1:1)

May the Lord Jesus strengthen my heart so that I will be blameless and holy in the presence of my God and Father when my Lord Jesus comes with all his holy ones. (1 Thess. 3:13)

God my Father loves me and by his grace gives me eternal encouragement and good hope. (2 Thess. 2:16)

Grace, mercy and peace come to me from God the Father and Christ Jesus my Lord. (1 Tim. 1:2)

64

Pleasing my Father

I should endure hardship as discipline; God is treating me as a son. For what son is not disciplined by his father? (Heb. 12:7)

I should submit to the Father of my spirit and live! (Heb. 12:9)

Every good and perfect gift is from above, coming down from the Father of the heavenly lights, who does not change like shifting shadows. (Jas. 1:17)

Religion that God my Father accepts as pure and faultless is this: to look after orphans and widows in their distress and to keep myself from being polluted by the world. (Jas. 1:27)

With my tongue I praise my Lord and Father. (Jas. 3:9)

I have been chosen according to the foreknowledge of God the Father, through the sanctifying work of the Spirit, for obedience to Jesus Christ and sprinkling by his blood. Grace and peace are mine in abundance. Praise be to the God and Father of my Lord Jesus Christ! In his great mercy he has given me new birth into a living hope through the resurrection of Jesus Christ from the dead. (1 Pet. 1: 2–3)

Since I call on a Father who judges each man's work impartially, I live my life as a stranger here in reverent fear. (1 Pet. 1:17)

65

My Father

My fellowship is with the Father and with his Son, Jesus Christ. (1 John 1:3)

If I sin, I have one who speaks to the Father in my defence – Jesus Christ, the Righteous One. (1 John 2:1)

Because I acknowledge the Son I have the Father also. If what I have heard from the beginning remains in me, I also will remain in the Son and in the Father. (1 John 2:23–4)

How great is the love the Father has lavished on me, that I should be called a child of God! And that is what I am! (1 John 3:1)

The Father has sent his Son to be the Saviour of the world. (1 John 4:14)

The Father commands me to walk in the truth. (2 John 1:4)

Because I continue in the teaching of Christ I have both the Father and the Son. (2 John 1:9)

Because I have been called, I am loved by God the Father and kept by Jesus Christ. (Jude v.1)

PART 5

Personal Revelation of Truth From the Epistles

Introduction

Much in the New Testament epistles lends itself to 'personalisation'. Paul and the other writers are not only writing to and about Christians of a bygone era; they are writing to you and about you personally, today!

Some of the material in this Part repeats themes covered in Part 2. However, the passages used will take us into these truths in greater depth. It will be simple for you to do your own personalisation of passages. This involves far less work than collecting verses around a particular theme, as in this Part. When you have read some of the following sections try personalising passages for yourself. This Part is a great help in this task because it is so important for every Christian to have a clear understanding of his position in Christ, of what God has done for him and what he enables the believer to do.

66

Called by God

I am among those who are called to belong to Jesus Christ. I am loved by God and called to be a saint. Grace and peace flow to me from God my Father and from the Lord Jesus Christ.

I am not ashamed of the gospel, because it is the power of God for the salvation of everyone who believes: *including me!* For in the gospel a righteousness from God is revealed to me, a righteousness that is by faith from first to last, just as it is written: 'The righteous will live by faith.'

No one will be declared righteous in God's sight by observing religious law; rather, the law makes me conscious of sin.

But now a righteousness from God, apart from law, has been made known to me, to which the Law and the Prophets testify. This righteousness from God comes through faith in Jesus Christ to all who believe, *including me!* I sinned and fell short of the glory of God; but I am justified freely by his grace through the redemption that came by Christ Jesus. God presented him as a sacrifice of atonement, through faith in his blood. He did this to demonstrate his justice, because in his forbearance he had left the sins committed beforehand unpunished – he did it to demonstrate his justice at the present time, so as to be just and the one who justifies those who have faith in Jesus, *including me!*

Am I able to boast then? No, my salvation has not come through observing the law, but through faith. I have been justified* by faith apart from observing the law.

(Rom. 1:6–7, 16–17; 3:20–8)

* To be justified is to be made righteous and totally acceptable to God. This is God's gift to everyone who is born again and comes through faith in Jesus as a work of God's grace.

67

Saved by Grace

As for me, I was dead in my transgressions and sins, in which I used to live when I followed the ways of this world and of the ruler of the kingdom of the air, the spirit who is now at work in those who are disobedient. I was one of them at one time, gratifying the cravings of my flesh and following its desires and thoughts. Like the rest, I was by nature an object of wrath. But because of his great love for me, God, who is rich in mercy, made me alive with Christ even when I was dead in transgressions – it is by grace I have been saved.

And God raised me up with Christ and seated me with him in the heavenly realms in Christ Jesus, in order that in the coming ages he might show the incomparable riches of his grace, expressed in his kindness to me in Christ Jesus. For it is by grace I have been saved, through faith – and this not from myself, it is the gift of God – not by works, so that I cannot boast. For I am God's workmanship, created in Christ Jesus to do good works, which God prepared in advance for me to do.

Once I was separate from Christ, excluded from citizenship in Israel and a foreigner to the covenants of promise. I was without hope and without God in the world. But now in Christ Jesus, I who once was far away have been brought near through the blood of Christ. For he himself is my peace.

(Eph. 2:1–10, 12–14)

68

Saved by his Grace

Grace and peace are mine from God my Father and the Lord Jesus Christ, who gave himself for my sins to rescue me from the present evil age, according to the will of my God and Father, to whom be glory for ever and ever. Amen.

I am not to desert the grace of Christ by turning to a different gospel – which is really no gospel at all. Some people cause confusion and try to pervert the gospel of Christ.

A man is not justified by observing the law, but by faith in Jesus Christ.* So I, too, have put my faith in Christ Jesus that I may be justified by faith in Christ and not by observing the law, because by observing the law no one will be justified.

God, who set me apart from birth and called me by his grace, was pleased to reveal his Son in me.

I have been crucified with Christ and I no longer live, but Christ lives with me. The life I live in the body, I live by faith in the Son of God, who loved me and gave himself for me. I do not set aside the grace of God, for if righteousness could be gained through the law, Christ died for nothing!

(Gal. 1:3–7; 2:15–16; 1:15; 2:20–1)

* There are many Scriptures which make it clear that no one is justified or made acceptable to God through obeying religious law or by any works of their own. It is only through personal faith in Jesus that anyone can be justified. Although in the New Testament the law refers to the law of the Old Testament, the same is true about those who try to please God by the observance of church law. No kind of religious exercise, performance or external actions can make a person acceptable to God; only faith in Jesus and his crucifixion can accomplish this.

69

Saved by his Grace (Cont.)

I have been justified through faith, and so I have peace with God through my Lord Jesus Christ, through whom I have gained access by faith into this grace in which I now stand. And I rejoice in the hope of the glory of God. Not only so, but I also rejoice in my sufferings, because I know that suffering produces perseverance; perseverance, character; and character, hope. And hope does not disappoint me, because God has poured out his love into my heart by the Holy Spirit, whom he has given me.

Christ died for me. But God has demonstrated his own love for me in this – while I was still a sinner, Christ died for me.

Since I have now been justified by his blood, how much more shall I be saved from God's wrath through him! For if, when I was God's enemy, I was reconciled to him through the death of his Son, how much more, having been reconciled, shall I be saved through his life! Not only is this so, but I also rejoice in God through my Lord Jesus Christ, through whom I have now received reconciliation.

By the trespass of Adam, death reigned through that one man. And I inherited that spiritual death. But now I have received God's abundant provision of grace and the gift of righteousness and can therefore reign in life through the one man, Jesus Christ.

Consequently, just as the result of one trespass was condemnation for me, so also the result of one act of righteousness by Jesus was justification* that brings me life. For just as through the disobedience of the one man I was made a sinner, so also through the obedience of the one man I am made righteous.

The law shows me my trespass. The more I am aware of my sin

* Justification means total acceptance by God.

the more I understand the amazing grace of God. That grace reigns through righteousness to bring me eternal life through Jesus Christ my Lord.

(Rom. 5:1–11, 17–21)

70

A Son of God

All who rely on observing the law are under a curse, for it is written: 'Cursed is everyone who does not continue to do everything written in the Book of the Law.' Clearly, no one is justified before God by the law, because 'The righteous will live by faith.' The law is not based on faith; on the contrary, 'The man who does these things will live by them.' Christ redeemed me from the curse of the law by becoming a curse for me, for it is written: 'Cursed is everyone who is hung on a tree.' He redeemed me in order that the blessing given to Abraham might come to the Gentiles through Christ Jesus, so that by faith I might receive the promise of the Spirit.

I am a son of God through faith in Christ Jesus, for I was baptised into Christ and have clothed myself with Christ. There is neither Jew nor Greek, slave nor free, male nor female, for we are all one in Christ Jesus. Because I belong to Christ, then I am Abraham's seed, and an heir according to the promise.

I was in slavery under the basic principles of the world. But when the time had fully come, God sent his Son, born of a woman, born under law, to redeem those under law, that I might receive the full rights of a son. Because I am a son, God sent the Spirit of his Son into my heart, the Spirit who calls out, 'Abba, Father.' So I am no longer a slave, but a son; and since I am a son, God has made me also an heir.

It is for freedom that Christ has set me free. I will stand firm, then, and will not let myself be burdened again by a yoke of slavery.

If I tried to be justified by religious law I would have been alienated from Christ; I would have fallen away from grace. But by faith I eagerly await through the Spirit the righteousness for which I hope. For in Christ Jesus the only thing that counts is faith expressing itself through love.

I was called to be free. But I am not to use my freedom to indulge the flesh; rather, I am to serve others in love.

(Gal. 3:10–14, 26–9; 4:3–7; 5:1, 4–6, 13)

71

Delivered from Law

I died to religious law through the body of Christ, that I might belong to another, to him who was raised from the dead, in order that I might bear fruit to God. For when I was controlled by the flesh, the sinful passions aroused by the law were at work in my body, so that I bore fruit for death. But now, by dying to what once bound me, I have been released from the law so that I serve in the new way of the Spirit, and not in the old way of religious legalism.

What shall I say, then? Is the law sin? Certainly not! Indeed I would not have known what sin was except through the law. For I would not have known what coveting really was if the law had not said, 'Do not covet.' But sin, seizing the opportunity afforded by the commandment, produced in me every kind of covetous desire. For apart from law, sin is dead. Once I was alive apart from law; but when the commandment came, sin sprang to life and I died. I found that the very commandment that was intended to bring life actually brought death. For sin, seizing the opportunity afforded by the commandment, deceived me, and through the commandment put me to death. So then, the law is holy, and the commandment is holy, righteous and good.

Did that which is good, then, become death to me? By no means! But in order that sin might be recognised as sin, it produced death in me through what was good, so that through the commandment sin might become utterly sinful.

I know that the law is spiritual; but I am unspiritual, sold as a slave to sin. I do not understand what I do. For what I want to do I do not do, but what I hate I do. And if I do what I do not want to do, I agree that the law is good. As it is, it is no longer I myself who do it, but it is sin living in me. I know that nothing good lives in me, that is, in my flesh. For I have the desire to do what is good, but I cannot carry it out. For what I do is not the good I want to do; no, the evil I do not want to do – this I keep on doing. Now if I do what I do not want to do, it is no longer I who do it, but it is sin living in me that does it.

So I find this law at work: when I want to do good, evil is right there with me. For in my inner being I delight in God's law; but I see another law at work in the members of my body, waging war against the law of my mind and making me a prisoner of the law of sin at work within my members. What a wretched man I am! Who will rescue me from this body of death? Thanks be to God – through Jesus Christ our Lord!

So then, I in my mind am a slave to God's law, but in the flesh I am a slave to the law of sin.

(Rom. 7:4–25)

72

Fullness in Christ

My purpose is that others may be encouraged in heart and united in love, so that they may have the full riches of complete understanding, in order that they may know the mystery of God, namely, Christ, in whom are hidden all the treasures of wisdom and knowledge.

So then, just as I received Christ Jesus as Lord, I am to continue to live in him, rooted and built up in him, strengthened in the faith as I was taught, and overflowing with thankfulness.

I will see to it no one takes me captive through hollow and deceptive philosophy, which depends on human tradition and the basic principles of this world rather than on Christ.

For in Christ all the fullness of the Deity lives in bodily form, and I have been given fullness in Christ, who is the Head over every power and authority. In him I was also circumcised, in the putting off of the flesh, not with a circumcision done by the hands of men but with the circumcision done by Christ, having been buried with him in baptism and raised with him through my faith in the power of God, who raised him from the dead.

When I was dead in my sins and in the uncircumcision of my flesh, God made me alive with Christ. He forgave me all my sins, having cancelled the written code, with its regulations, that was against me and that stood opposed to me; he took it away, nailing it to the cross. And having disarmed the powers and authorities, he made a public spectacle of them, triumphing over them by the cross.

Since I have been raised with Christ, I choose to set my heart on things above, where Christ is seated at the right hand of God. I set my mind on things above, not on earthly things. For I died, and my life is now hidden with Christ in God. When Christ, who is my life, appears, then I also will appear with him in glory.

I put to death, therefore, whatever belongs to my earthly nature: sexual immorality, impurity, lust, evil desires and greed, which is idolatry. Because of these, the wrath of God is coming on those who are disobedient. I used to walk in these ways, in the life I once lived. But now I must rid myself of all such things as these: anger, rage, malice, slander and filthy language from my lips. I do not lie to others, since I have taken off my old self with its practices and have put on the new self, which is being renewed in knowledge in the image of its creator.

(Col. 2:2–3, 6–7, 9–15; 3:1–10)

73

I am in Christ

I am a servant of Christ Jesus by the will of God. He has made me a saint, one of the faithful, living in Christ Jesus. Grace and peace is poured into my life from God my Father and the Lord Jesus Christ.

I praise my God and Father, the Father of my Lord, Jesus Christ. He has blessed me in the heavenly realms with every spiritual blessing in Christ. For he chose me in him before the creation of the world to be holy and blameless in his sight. In love he predestined me to be adopted as his son through Jesus Christ, in accordance with his pleasure and will – to the praise of his glorious grace, which he has freely given me in the one he loves.

In him I have redemption through his blood, the forgiveness of my sins, in accordance with the riches of God's grace that he lavished on me with all wisdom and understanding. And he made known to me the mystery of his will according to his good pleasure, which he purposed in Christ, to be put into effect when the times reach their fulfilment – to bring all things in heaven and on earth together under one head, even Christ.

In him I was also chosen, having been predestined according to the plan of him who works out everything in conformity with the purpose of his will, in order that I, who have put my hope in Christ, might be for the praise of his glory. And I was included in Christ when I heard the word of truth, the gospel of my salvation. Having believed, I was marked in him with a seal, the promised Holy Spirit, who is a deposit guaranteeing my inheritance until the redemption of those who are God's possession – to the praise of his glory.

(Eph. 1:1–14)

74

Resurrection

If Christ has not been raised, my faith is futile; I would still be in my sins. Then those also who have fallen asleep in Christ are lost. If only for this life I have hope in Christ, I am to be pitied more than all men.

But Christ has indeed been raised from the dead, the first fruits of those who have fallen asleep. For since death came through a man, the resurrection of the dead comes also through a man. For as in Adam I died, so in Christ I have been made alive.

At the resurrection of the dead, my perishable body is to be raised imperishable; my body, sown in dishonour, is to be raised in glory. What is sown in weakness is raised in power; it is sown a natural body, it is raised a spiritual body. If I have a natural body, I will also have a spiritual body.

Just as I have borne the likeness of the earthly man, so I shall bear the likeness of the man from heaven. My flesh and blood cannot inherit the kingdom of God, nor does the perishable inherit the imperishable.

I reveal this mystery: we will not all sleep, but we will all be changed – in a flash, in the twinkling of an eye, at the last trumpet. For the trumpet will sound, I will be raised imperishable, and I will be changed.

Thanks be to God! He gives me the victory through my Lord Jesus Christ. Therefore, I stand firm. Nothing moves me. I always give myself fully to the work of the Lord, because I know that my labour in the Lord is not in vain.

I am to be on my guard; to stand firm in the faith; to be a person of courage; I am to be strong. I am to do everything in love. The grace of the Lord Jesus is with me. I am to love all who are in Christ Jesus.

(1 Cor. 15:17–22, 42–4, 49–52, 57–8; 16:13–14, 23–4)

75

A New Creation

I have a building from God, an eternal house in heaven, not built by human hands. Meanwhile I groan, longing to be clothed with my heavenly dwelling, because when I am clothed, I will not be found naked.

For while I am in this tent, I groan and am burdened, because I do not wish to be unclothed but to be clothed with my heavenly dwelling, so that what is mortal may be swallowed up by life. Now it is God who has made me for this very purpose and has given me the Spirit as a deposit, guaranteeing what is to come.

Therefore I am always confident and know that as long as I am at home in the body I am away from the Lord. I live by faith, not by sight. I am confident, I say, and would prefer to be away from the body and at home with the Lord.

So I make it my goal to please him, whether I am at home in the body or away from it. For I must appear before the judgment seat of Christ, that I may receive what is due to me for the things done while in the body, whether good or bad.

Since, then, I know what it is to fear the Lord, I try to persuade men. What I am is plain to God, and I hope it is also plain to others.

Christ's love compels me, because I am convinced that one died for me, and therefore I died. And he died for me that I should no longer live for myself but for him who died for me and was raised again.

So from now on I regard no one from a worldly point of view. Though I once regarded Christ in this way, I do so no longer. Therefore, because I am in Christ, I am a new creation; the old has gone, the new has come!

All this is from God, who reconciled me to himself through Christ and gave me the ministry of reconciliation: that God was reconciling the world to himself in Christ, not counting men's sins against them. And he has committed to me the message of reconciliation. I am therefore Christ's ambassador, as though God were making his appeal through me. I implore you on Christ's behalf: be reconciled to God.

God made him who had no sin to be sin for me, so that in him I might become the righteousness of God.

(2 Cor. 5:1–11, 14–21)

76

Dead and Buried with Christ

What shall I say, then? Shall I go on sinning, so that grace may increase? By no means! I died to sin; how can I live in it any longer? Because I was baptised into Christ Jesus, I was baptised into his death. I was therefore buried with him through baptism into death in order that, just as Christ was raised from the dead through the glory of the Father, I too may live a new life.

If I have been united with him like this in his death, I will certainly also be united with him in his resurrection. For I know that my old self was crucified with him so that the body of sin might be done away with, that I should no longer be a slave to sin – because anyone who has died has been freed from sin.

Now if I died with Christ, I believe that I will also live with him. For I know that since Christ was raised from the dead, he cannot die again; death no longer has mastery over him. The death he died, he died to sin once for all; but the life he lives, he lives to God.

In the same way, I count myself dead to sin but alive to God in Christ Jesus. Therefore I do not let sin reign in my mortal body so that I obey its evil desires. I do not offer the parts of my body to sin, as instruments of wickedness, but rather I offer myself to God, as one who has been brought from death to life; and I offer the parts of my body to him as instruments of righteousness. For sin shall not be my master, because I am not under law, but under grace. What then? Shall I sin because I am not under law but under grace?

By no means! I know that I am a slave to the one whom I obey – whether I am a slave to sin, which leads to death, or to obedience, which leads to righteousness. But thanks be to God that, though I used to be a slave to sin, I wholeheartedly obeyed the form of teaching to which I was entrusted. I have been set free from sin and have become a slave to righteousness.

I am weak in my natural self. Just as I used to offer the parts of my body in slavery to impurity and to ever-increasing wickedness, so now I offer them in slavery to righteousness leading to holiness. When I was a slave to sin, I was free from the control of righteousness. What benefit did I reap at that time from the things I am now ashamed of? Those things result in death! But now that I have been set free from sin and have become a slave to God, the benefit I reap leads to holiness, and the result is eternal life. For the wages of sin is death, but the gift of God to me is eternal life in Christ Jesus our Lord.

(Rom. 6:1–23)

77

My Salvation

I have been chosen according to the foreknowledge of God the Father, through the sanctifying work of the Spirit, for obedience to Jesus Christ and sprinkling by his blood. Grace and peace are mine in abundance.

I praise the God and Father of my Lord Jesus Christ! In his great mercy he has given me new birth into a living hope through the resurrection of Jesus Christ from the dead, and into an inheritance that can never perish, spoil or fade – kept in heaven for me, who through faith am shielded by God's power until the coming of the salvation that is ready to be revealed in the last time.

In this I greatly rejoice, though now for a little while I may have had to suffer grief through all kinds of trials. These have come so that my faith – of greater worth than gold, which perishes even though refined by fire – may be proved genuine and may result in praise, glory and honour when Jesus Christ is revealed.

Though I have not seen him, I love him; and even though I do not see him now, I believe in him and am filled with an inexpressible and glorious joy, for I am receiving the goal of my faith, the salvation of my soul.

Concerning this salvation, the prophets, who spoke of the grace that was to come to me, searched intently and with the greatest care, trying to find out the time and circumstances to which the Spirit of Christ in them was pointing when he predicted the sufferings of Christ and the glories that would follow. It was revealed to them that they were not serving themselves but me, when they spoke of the things that have now been told to me by those who have preached the gospel to me by the Holy Spirit sent from heaven. Even angels long to look into these things.

Therefore, I prepare my mind for action; I am to be self-controlled; I set my hope fully on the grace to be given to me when Jesus Christ is revealed. As an obedient child, I do not conform to the evil desires

I had when I lived in ignorance. But just as he who called me is holy, so I am to be holy in all I do; for it is written: 'Be holy, because I am holy.'

(1 Pet. 1:2, 3–16)

78

Made Perfect For Ever

I have a high priest, who sat down at the right hand of the throne of the Majesty in heaven.

By God's will, I have been made holy through the sacrifice of the body of Jesus Christ once for all. By his one sacrifice he has made me perfect for ever.*

Therefore, I have confidence to enter the most holy place by the blood of Jesus, by a new and living way opened for me through the curtain, that is, his body, and since I have a great priest over the house of God, I can draw near to God with a sincere heart in full assurance of faith, having my heart sprinkled to cleanse me from a guilty conscience and having my body washed with pure water. I am able to hold unswervingly to the hope I profess, for he who promised me is faithful. I can consider how I am able to spur others on towards love and good deeds. I will not give up meeting others, as some are in the habit of doing, but will encourage others – and all the more as I see the Day approaching.

I will not throw away my confidence; it will be richly rewarded. I need to persevere so that when I have done the will of God, I will receive what he has promised me. For in just a very little while, 'He who is coming will come and will not delay. But my righteous one will live by faith. And if he shrinks back, I will not be pleased with him.' But I am not of those who shrink back and am destroyed; I believe and am saved.

(Heb. 8:1; 10:10, 14, 19–25, 35–9)

* The writer of this epistle makes it clear that in my spirit I am made holy and perfect for ever. However, I do not yet manifest that perfection completely in my soul life yet. In my soul I am being transformed into the likeness of Jesus from one degree of glory to another. I need to keep my soul submitted to the Spirit of God so that his presence and life within me can be expressed more and more fully. The good news is that even when I sin I do not lose the holiness and perfection that is mine in Christ.

79

The Goal

I rejoice in the Lord! This is a safeguard for me. Because I worship by the Spirit of God, and glory in Christ Jesus, I put no confidence in the flesh.*

Whatever was to my profit I now consider loss for the sake of Christ. What is more, I consider everything a loss compared to the surpassing greatness of knowing Christ Jesus, my Lord, for whose sake I have lost all things. I consider them rubbish, that I may gain Christ and be found in him, not having a righteousness of my own that comes from the law, but that which is through faith in Christ – the righteousness that comes from God and is by faith. I want to know Christ and the power of his resurrection and the fellowship of sharing in his sufferings, becoming like him in his death, and so, somehow, to attain to the resurrection from the dead.

Not that I have already obtained all this, or have already been made perfect, but I press on to take hold of that for which Christ Jesus took hold of me. Brothers, I do not consider myself yet to have taken hold of it. But this one thing I do: forgetting what is behind and straining towards what is ahead, I press on towards the goal to win the prize for which God has called me heavenwards in Christ Jesus.

All of us who are mature should take such a view of things. And if on some point you think differently, that, too, God will make clear to you.

(Phil. 3:1, 3, 7–15)

* This is a direct quotation from Philippians. You can identify with these words of Paul.

80

Living in the Spirit

There is now no condemnation for me because I am in Christ Jesus, and I do not live according to the flesh but according to the Spirit.* Through Christ Jesus the law of the Spirit of life set me free from the law of sin and death. For what the law was powerless to do in that it was weakened by the flesh, God did by sending his own Son in the likeness of sinful man to be an offering to sin. And so he condemned sin in sinful man, in order that the righteous requirements of the law might be fully met in me, who do not live according to the flesh but according to the Spirit.

If I live according to the flesh I have my mind set on what my flesh desires; but if I live in accordance with the Spirit I have my mind set on what the Spirit desires. The mind of sinful man is death, but the mind controlled by the Spirit is life and peace; the sinful mind is hostile to God. It does not submit to God's law, nor can it do so. Those controlled by the flesh cannot please God.

I, however, am controlled not by my flesh but by the Spirit, because the Spirit of God lives in me. And if anyone does not have the Spirit of Christ, he does not belong to Christ. Because Christ is in me, my body is dead because of sin, yet my spirit is alive because of righteousness. And if the Spirit of him who raised Jesus from the dead is living in me, he who raised Christ from the dead will also give life to my mortal body through his Spirit, who lives in me.

I have an obligation – but it is not to live according to my flesh. For if I live according to my flesh, I will die; but if by the Spirit I put to death the misdeeds of the body, I will live, because if I am led by the Spirit of God, I am a son of God.

For I did not receive a spirit that makes me a slave again to fear,

* You will notice that in this and other passages the N.I.V. phrase 'the sinful nature' has been replaced by the word 'flesh', which is a more faithful translation of the word used in the original Greek.

but I received the Spirit of sonship. And through him I cry, 'Abba, Father'. The Spirit himself testifies with my spirit that I am God's child. Now if I am his child, then I am his heir – an heir of God and a co-heir with Christ, if indeed I share in his sufferings in order that I may also share in his glory.

I consider that my present sufferings are not worth comparing with the glory that will be revealed in me.

(Rom. 8:1–18)

81

Temple of the Holy Spirit

I am a servant of Christ and am entrusted with the secret things of God. It is required of me that as I have been given a trust I must prove faithful. When the Lord comes, he will bring to light what is hidden in darkness and will expose the motives of my heart. At that time I will receive praise from God.

What makes me different from anyone else? What do I have that I did not receive? And if I did receive it, why do I boast as though I did not?

I have been washed, I have been sanctified, I have been justified in the name of the Lord Jesus Christ and by the Spirit of my God.

'Everything is permissible for me' – but not everything is beneficial. 'Everything is permissible for me' – but I will not be mastered by anything. My body is not meant for sexual immorality, but for the Lord, and the Lord for my body.

By his power God raised the Lord from the dead, and he will raise me also. I know that my body is a member of Christ himself. Shall I then take a member of Christ and unite it with a prostitute? Never! I have united myself with the Lord, and am one with him in spirit. I know that my body is a temple of the Holy Spirit, who is in me, whom I have received from God. I am not my own; I was bought at a price. Therefore, I honour God with my body.

'Everything is permissible' – but not everything is beneficial. 'Everything is permissible' – but not everything is constructive. I should seek not my own good, but the good of others.

(1 Cor. 4:1–2, 5, 7; 6:11–15, 17, 19–20; 10:23–4)

82

Live by the Spirit

The entire law is summed up in a single command: 'Love your neighbour as yourself.' If I keep on biting and devouring others, I had better watch out or I will be destroyed by others.

But if I live by the Spirit I will not gratify the desires of the flesh. For the flesh desires what is contrary to the Spirit, and the Spirit what is contrary to the flesh. They are in conflict with each other, so that I do not do what I want. But if I am led by the Spirit, I am not under law.

The acts of the flesh are obvious: sexual immorality, impurity and debauchery; idolatry and witchcraft; hatred, discord, jealousy, fits of rage, selfish ambition, dissensions, factions and envy; drunkenness, orgies, and the like. I warn you, as I did before, that those who live like this will not inherit the kingdom of God.

But the fruit of the Spirit is love, joy, peace, patience, kindness, goodness, faithfulness, gentleness and self-control. Against such things there is no law. As one who belongs to Christ Jesus I have crucified the flesh with its passions and desires. Since I live by the Spirit, I will keep in step with the Spirit. I am not to become conceited, provoking and envying others.

Brothers, if someone is caught in a sin, I who am spiritual should restore him gently. But I am to watch myself, or I also may be tempted. I will carry others' burdens, and in this way I will fulfil the law of Christ. If I think I am something when I am nothing, I deceive myself. I should test my own actions. Then I can take pride in myself, without comparing myself to somebody else, for I should carry my own load.

When I receive instruction in the word I must share all good things with my instructor. I am not to be deceived: God cannot be mocked. I reap what I sow. If I sow to please my flesh, from that flesh I will reap destruction; if I sow to please the Spirit, from the Spirit I will reap eternal life. I will not become weary in doing good, for at the proper time I will reap a harvest if I do not give up. Therefore, as I have opportunity, I will do good to all people, especially to those who belong to the family of believers.

(Gal. 5:14–26; 6:1–10)

83

Christ my Foundation

I have not received the spirit of the world but the Spirit who is from God, that I may understand what God has freely given me. The man without the Spirit does not accept the things that come from the Spirit of God, for they are foolishness to him, and he cannot understand them, because they are spiritually discerned.

As a spiritual person I am able to make judgments about all things, and am myself not subject to any man's judgment: I have the mind of Christ.

The foundation of my life is Jesus Christ. If I build on this foundation using gold, silver, costly stones, wood, hay or straw, my work will be shown for what it is, because the Day will bring it to light. It will be revealed with fire, and the fire will test the quality of my work. If what I have built survives, I will receive my reward. If it is burned up, I will suffer loss; I myself will be saved, but only as one escaping through the flames.

I am God's temple and God's Spirit lives in me. If anyone destroys God's temple, God will destroy him; for God's temple is sacred, and I am that temple. I will not be deceived. I will not boast about men! All things are mine, whether Paul or Apollos or Cephas or the world or life or death or the present or the future – all are mine, and I am of Christ, and Christ is of God.

(1 Cor. 2:12, 14–16; 3:11–18, 21–3)

84

Everything I Need

Through the righteousness of my God and Saviour Jesus Christ I have received a faith as precious as that of the apostles. Grace and peace are mine in abundance through the knowledge of God and of Jesus our Lord.

His divine power has given me everything I need for life and godliness through my knowledge of him who called me by his own glory and goodness. Through these he has given me his very great and precious promises, so that through them I may participate in the divine nature and escape the corruption in the world caused by evil desires.

For this very reason, I make every effort to add goodness to my faith; and to goodness, knowledge; and to knowledge, self-control; and to self-control, perseverance; and to perseverance, godliness; and to godliness, brotherly kindness; and to brotherly kindness, love. For if I possess these qualities in increasing measure, they will keep me from being ineffective and unproductive in my knowledge of our Lord Jesus Christ. But if I do not have them, I am short-sighted and blind, and have forgotten that I have been cleansed from my past sins.

Therefore, I am all the more eager to make my calling and election sure. For if I do these things, I will never fall, and I will receive a rich welcome into the eternal kingdom of our Lord and Saviour Jesus Christ.

(2 Pet. 1:1–11)

85

The Attitude of Christ

I am encouraged by being united with Christ; I receive comfort from his love; I have fellowship with the Spirit; I know his tenderness and compassion. And so I want to give joy to my Father by being like-minded with other believers, having the same love, being one in spirit and purpose. I will do nothing out of selfish ambition or vain conceit, but in humility I consider others better than myself. I will look not only to my own interests, but also to the interests of others.

My attitude will be the same as that of Christ Jesus. He, who, being in very nature God, did not consider equality with God something to be grasped, but made himself nothing, taking the very nature of a servant, being made in human likeness. And being found in appearance as a man, he humbled himself and became obedient to death – even death on a cross! Therefore God exalted him to the highest place and gave him the name that is above every name, that at the name of Jesus every knee should bow, in heaven and on earth and under the earth, and every tongue confess that Jesus Christ is Lord, to the glory of God the Father.

Therefore, as I have always sought to obey – I continue to work out my salvation with fear and trembling, for it is God who works in me to will and to act according to his good purpose.

I am to do everything without complaining or arguing, so that I may become blameless and pure, a child of God without fault in a crooked and depraved generation, in which I shine like a star in the universe as I hold out the word of life – in order that I may boast on the day of Christ that I did not run or labour for nothing.

(Phil. 2:1–16)

86

Redeemed

Since I call on a Father who judges each man's work impartially, I live my life as a stranger here in reverent fear. For I know that it was not with perishable things such as silver or gold that I was redeemed from the empty way of life handed down to me from my forefathers, but with the precious blood of Christ, a lamb without blemish or defect. He was chosen before the creation of the world, but was revealed in these last times for my sake. Through him I believe in God, who raised him from the dead and glorified him, and so my faith and hope are in God.

Now that I have purified myself by obeying the truth so that I have sincere love for my brothers, I love others deeply, from the heart. For I have been born again, not of perishable seed, but of imperishable, through the living and enduring word of God. For, it is written, 'All men are like grass, and all their glory is like the flowers of the field; the grass withers and the flowers fall, but the word of the Lord stands for ever.' And this is the word that was preached to me.

Therefore, I rid myself of all malice and all deceit, hypocrisy, envy, and slander of every kind. Like a newborn babe, I crave pure spiritual milk, so that by it I may grow up in my salvation, now that I have tasted that the Lord is good.

As I come to him, the living stone – rejected by men but chosen by God and precious to him – I also, like a living stone, am being built into a spiritual house to be a holy priest, offering spiritual sacrifices acceptable to God through Jesus Christ.

I am a chosen person, a royal priest. I am part of a holy nation, a people belonging to God, that I may declare the praises of him who called me out of darkness into his wonderful light. Once I was not one of his people, but now I am one of the people of God; once I had not received mercy, but now I have received mercy.

(1 Pet. 1:17–25; 2:1–5, 9–10)

87

Always Joyful

I rejoice in the Lord always. The Lord reminds me again and again: Rejoice! I want my gentleness to be evident to all. The Lord is near me. I will not be anxious about anything, but in everything, by prayer and petition, with thanksgiving, present my requests to God. And the peace of God, which transcends all understanding, will guard my heart and my mind in Christ Jesus.

Whatever is true, whatever is noble, whatever is right, whatever is pure, whatever is lovely, whatever is admirable – if anything is excellent or praiseworthy – I will think about such things. Whatever I have learned or received or heard through God's word, or seen in godly people, I will put into practice. And the God of peace will be with me.

I have learned to be content whatever the circumstances. I know what it is to be in need, and I know what it is to have plenty. I have learned the secret of being content in any and every situation, whether well fed or hungry, whether living in plenty or in want. I can do everything through him who gives me strength.

And my God will meet all my needs according to his glorious riches in Christ Jesus. To my God and Father be glory for ever and ever. Amen.

(Phil. 4:4–9, 11–13, 19, 20)

88

Faith

Faith is being sure of what I hope for and certain of what I do not see. This is what the ancients were commended for.

Without faith it is impossible for me to please God, because when I come to him I must believe that he exists and that he rewards me for earnestly seeking him.

Since I am surrounded by such a great cloud of witnesses, I am to throw off everything that hinders and the sin that so easily entangles, and run with perseverance the race marked out for me. I fix my eyes on Jesus, that author and perfecter of my faith, who for the joy set before him endured the cross, scorning its shame, and sat down at the right hand of the throne of God. I consider him who endured such opposition from sinful men, so that I will not grow weary and lose heart.

I am to consider it pure joy whenever I face trials of many kinds, because I know that the testing of my faith develops perseverance. Perseverance must finish its work so that I may be mature and complete, not lacking anything. If I lack wisdom, I should ask God, who gives generously to all without finding fault, and it will be given to me. But when I ask, I must believe and not doubt, because if I doubt I am like a wave of the sea, blown and tossed by the wind. In which case I should not think I will receive anything from the Lord; I would be a double-minded man, unstable in all I do.

I am blessed when I persevere under trial, because when I have stood the test, I will receive the crown of life that God has promised to me because I love him.

My faith by itself, if it is not accompanied by action, is dead.

(Heb. 11:1, 6; 12:1–15; Jas. 1:2–8, 12; 2:17)

89

The Word of Faith

The Word is near me; it is in my mouth and in my heart, that is, the Word of faith I proclaim. If I confess with my mouth, 'Jesus is Lord' and believe in my heart that God raised him from the dead, I will be saved. For it is with my heart that I believe and am justified, and it is with my mouth that I confess and am saved.

If I trust in him I will never be put to shame! I have called on the name of the Lord and am saved. Faith has come to me from hearing the message, and I have heard the message through the word of Christ.

The promise of entering his rest still stands. So I must be careful that I am not found to have fallen short of it. The message of the gospel is of no value to me, unless when I hear it I combine it with faith. Because I have believed I enter that rest.

The Word of God is living and active. Sharper than any double-edged sword, it penetrates even to dividing my soul and spirit, joints and marrow; it judges the thoughts and attitudes of my heart. Nothing in all my life is hidden from God's sight. Everything is uncovered and laid bare before the eyes of him to whom I must give account.

Therefore, since I have a great high priest who has gone through the heavens, Jesus the Son of God, I hold firmly to the faith I profess. For I do not have a high priest who is unable to sympathise with my weaknesses, but I have one who has been tempted in every way, just as I am – yet was without sin.

Therefore, I can approach the throne of grace with confidence, so that I may receive mercy and find grace to help me in my time of need.

(Rom. 10:8–11, 13, 17; Heb. 4:1–3, 12–16)

90

The Spirit of Faith

The god of this age has blinded the minds of unbelievers, so that they cannot see the light of the gospel of the glory of Christ, who is the image of God. For God, who said, 'Let light shine out of darkness' made his light shine in my heart to give me the light of the knowledge of the glory of God in the face of Christ. But I have this treasure in a jar of clay to show that this all-surpassing power is from God and not from me.

I am hard pressed on every side, but not crushed; perplexed, but not in despair; persecuted, but not abandoned; struck down, but not destroyed. I always carry around in my body the death of Jesus, so that the life of Jesus may also be revealed in my body.

For I who am alive am always being given over to death for Jesus's sake, so that his life may be revealed in my mortal body. So then, death is at work in me, but life is at work in others.

It is written: 'I believed; therefore I have spoken.' With that same spirit of faith I also believe and therefore speak, because I know that the one who raised the Lord Jesus from the dead will also raise me with Jesus and present me with others in his presence. All this is for the benefit of others, so that the grace that is reaching more and more people may cause thanksgiving to overflow to the glory of God. Therefore, I do not lose heart. Though outwardly I am wasting away, yet inwardly I am being renewed day by day. For my light and momentary troubles are achieving for me an eternal glory that far outweighs them all. So I fix my eyes not on what is seen, but on what is unseen. For what is seen is temporary, but what is unseen is eternal.

(2 Cor. 4:4, 6–18)

91

Living in the Truth

I do not believe every spirit, but test the spirits to see whether they are from God, because many false prophets have gone out into the world. This is how I can recognise the Spirit of God: every spirit that acknowledges that Jesus Christ has come in the flesh is from God, but every spirit that does not acknowledge Jesus is not from God. This is the spirit of the antichrist, which I have heard is coming and even now is already in the world.

I am born of God and have overcome them, because the one who is in me is greater than the one who is in the world. They are from the world and therefore speak from the viewpoint of the world, and the world listens to them. I am from God, and whoever knows God listens to me; but whoever is not from God does not listen to me. This is how I recognise the Spirit of truth and the spirit of falsehood.

I know that anyone born of God does not continue to sin; the one who was born of God keeps me safe, and the evil one cannot harm me. I know that I am a child of God, and that the whole world is under the control of the evil one. I know also that the Son of God has come and has given me understanding, so that I may know him who is true. And I am in him who is true – even in his Son Jesus Christ. He is the true God and eternal life. And so I keep myself from idols.

God has given me eternal life, and this life is in his Son. Because I have the Son I have life; he who does not have the Son of God does not have life.

I believe in the name of the Son of God and know that I have eternal life. This is the confidence I have in approaching God: that if I ask anything according to his will, he hears me. And if I know that he hears me – whatever I ask – I know that I have what I asked of him.

(1 John 4:1–6, 18–21, 11–15)

92

Increasing Faith and Love

My faith is growing more and more, and the love I have for others is increasing. I am learning to persevere in faith in all the persecutions and trials I endure.

All this is evidence that God's judgment is right, and as a result I will be counted worthy of the kingdom of God, for which I am suffering. God is just. He will pay back trouble to those who trouble me and give relief to me when troubled. This will happen when the Lord Jesus is revealed from heaven in blazing fire with his powerful angels. He will punish those who do not know God and do not obey the gospel of the Lord Jesus. They will be punished with everlasting destruction and shut out from the presence of the Lord and from the majesty of his power on the day he comes to be glorified in his holy people and to be marvelled at among all those who have believed. This includes me, because I believed the gospel.

I pray that my God may count me worthy of his calling, and that by his power he may fulfil every good purpose of mine and every act prompted by my faith. I pray this so that the name of my Lord Jesus may be glorified in me, and I in him, according to the grace of my God and the Lord Jesus Christ.

I am loved by the Lord, because from the beginning God chose me to be saved through the sanctifying work of the Spirit and through belief in truth. He called me to this through the gospel, that I might share in the glory of my Lord Jesus Christ. So then, brothers, I stand firm and hold to the teachings I received, whether by word of mouth or the written word.

May my Lord Jesus Christ himself and God my Father, who loves me and by his grace gave me eternal encouragement and good hope, encourage my heart and strengthen me in every good deed and word.

(2 Thess. 1:3–17)

93

True Fellowship

My fellowship is with the Father and his son, Jesus Christ. He wants to make my joy complete.

This is the message I have heard from him and declare to others: God is light; in him there is no darkness at all. If I claim to have fellowship with him yet walk in the darkness, I lie and do not live by the truth. But if I walk in the light, as he is in the light, I have fellowship with others, and the blood of Jesus, his Son, purifies me from all sin.

If I claim to be without sin, I deceive myself and the truth is not in me. If I confess my sins, he is faithful and just and will forgive me my sins and purify me from all unrighteousness. If I claim I have not sinned, I make him out to be a liar and his Word has no place in my life.

I am to take note of these things so that I will not sin. But if I do sin, I have one who speaks to the Father in my defence – Jesus Christ, the Righteous One. He is the atoning sacrifice for my sins, and not only mine but also for the sins of the whole world.

I know that I have come to know him if I obey his commands. If I were to say, 'I know him' but not do what he commands I would be a liar, and the truth would not be in me. But if I obey his Word, God's love is truly made complete in me. This is how I know I am in him: because I claim to live in him I must walk as Jesus did.

(1 John 1:3–10, 2:1–6)

94

The Boldness of Love

God my Father and the Lord Jesus Christ give me grace and peace. He who began a good work in me will carry it on to completion until the day of Christ Jesus.

My prayer is that my love may abound more and more in knowledge and depth of insight, so that I may be able to discern what is best and may be pure and blameless until the day of Christ, filled with the fruit of righteousness that comes through Jesus Christ – to the glory and praise of God.

I realise that what has happened to me has really served to advance the gospel. I am encouraged to speak the Word of God more courageously and fearlessly. I will not preach Christ out of envy and rivalry, but out of goodwill. I will do so in love, knowing that I am here for the defence of the gospel. I will not preach Christ out of selfish ambition, or with insincerity.

I believe God will give me sufficient courage so that Christ will always be exalted in my body, whether by life or by death. For to me, to live is Christ and to die is gain. If I am to go on living in the body, this will mean fruitful labour for me.

Whatever happens, I will conduct myself in a manner worthy of the gospel of Christ. I will stand firm in the Spirit, contending with others for the faith of the gospel without being frightened in any way by those who oppose me. For it has been granted to me on behalf of Christ not only to believe in him, but also to suffer for him.

(Phil. 1:1, 6, 9–12, 14, 16–17, 20–2, 27–9)

95

My Prayer

Lord Jesus, thank you for being the author of my faith and for giving me love for all the saints. Heavenly Father, you are the Lord of glory. Please give me the Spirit of wisdom and revelation, so that I may know you better.

I pray also that the eyes of my heart may be enlightened in order that I may know the hope to which I have been called by you, the riches of my glorious inheritance in the saints, and your incomparably great power for me because I believe. That power is like the working of your mighty strength, which you exerted in Christ when you raised him from the dead and seated him at your right hand in the heavenly realms, far above all rule and authority, power and dominion, and every title that can be given, not only in the present age but also in the one to come.

And Father, you placed all things under his feet and appointed him to be head over everything for the church, which is his body, the fullness of him who fills everything in every way. And I rejoice to be alive in him!

I pray that out of your glorious riches you will strengthen me with power through your Spirit in my inner being, so that Christ may dwell in my heart through faith. And I pray that being rooted and established in love, I may have power, together with all the saints, to grasp how wide and long and high and deep is the love of Christ for me, and to know this love that surpasses knowledge – that I may be filled to the measure of all your fullness of life.

You are able to do immeasurably more than all I ask or imagine, according to your power that is at work within me. Be glorified in your Church and in Christ Jesus throughout all generations, for ever and ever! Amen.

(Eph. 1:15–23; 3:16–21)

96

Practical Love

My love must be sincere. I hate what is evil; I cling to what is good. I am to be devoted to others in brotherly love. I will honour others above myself. I intend never to be lacking in zeal, but to keep my spiritual fervour, serving the Lord. I will be joyful in hope, patient in affliction, faithful in prayer. I will share with God's people who are in need. I will practise hospitality.

I will bless those who persecute me; I will bless and not curse them. I will rejoice with those who rejoice; I will mourn with those who mourn. I will live in harmony with others. I will not be proud, but am willing to associate with people of low position. I will not be conceited.

I will not repay anyone evil for evil. I will be careful to do what is right in the eyes of everybody. If it is possible, as far as it depends on me, I will live at peace with everyone. I will not take revenge, but will leave room for God's wrath, for it is written: 'It is mine to avenge; I will repay,' says the Lord. On the contrary: 'If my enemy is hungry, I will feed him; if he is thirsty, I will give him something to drink.' In doing this, I will heap burning coals on his head.

I will let no debt remain outstanding, except the continuing debt to love others, for if I love my fellow man I have fulfilled the law.

I clothe myself with the Lord Jesus Christ, and do not think about how to gratify the desires of my flesh.

(Rom. 12:1–6, 9–20; 13:8, 14)

97

Dealing with Opposition

The end of all things is near. Therefore I am to be clear minded and self-controlled so that I can pray. Above all, I am to love others deeply, because love covers over a multitude of sins.

I need to offer hospitality to others without grumbling. I should use whatever gift I have received to serve others, faithfully administering God's grace in its various forms. If I speak, I should do it as one speaking the very words of God. If I serve, I should do it with the strength God provides, so that in all things God may be praised through Jesus Christ. To him be the glory and the power for ever and ever. Amen.

I should not be surprised at the painful trial I suffer, as though something strange were happening to me. Rather I rejoice that I participate in the sufferings of Christ, so that I may be overjoyed when his glory is revealed. If I am insulted because of the name of Christ, I am blessed, for the Spirit of glory and of God rests on me. If I suffer, it should not be as a murderer or thief or any other kind of criminal, or even as a meddler. However, if I suffer as a Christian, I should not be ashamed, but praise God that I bear that name.

Though I live in the world, I do not wage war as the world does. The weapons I fight with are not the weapons of the world. On the contrary, they have divine power to demolish strongholds. I demolish arguments and every pretension that sets itself up against the knowledge of God, and I take captive every thought to make it obedient to Christ.

God's grace is sufficient for me, for his power is made perfect in weakness. I will boast all the more gladly about my weaknesses, so that Christ's power may rest on me. That is why, for Christ's sake, I delight in weaknesses, in insults, in hardships, in persecutions, in difficulties. For when I am weak, then I am strong.

I am weak in him, yet by God's power I will live with him to serve others.

(1 Pet. 4:7–16; 2 Cor. 12:9–10; 13:4)

98

I am Loved

The Spirit helps me in my weakness. I do not know what I ought to pray for, but the Spirit himself intercedes for me with groans that words cannot express. And he who searches my heart knows the mind of the Spirit, because the Spirit intercedes for me in accordance with God's will.

And I know that in all things God works for my good because I love him and have been called according to his purpose. God foreknew me and also predestined me to be conformed to the likeness of his Son, that he might be the firstborn among many brothers. He not only predestined me, he also called me; he not only called me, he also justified me; he not only justified me, he also glorified me.

What, then, shall I say in response to this? If God is for me, who can be against me? He who did not spare his own Son, but gave him up for me – how will he not also, along with him, graciously give me all things? Who will bring any charge against me, for God has chosen me? God has justified me. Who is he that condemns? Christ Jesus, who died – more than that, who was raised to life – is at the right hand of God and is also interceding for me. Who shall separate me from the love of Christ? Shall trouble or hardship or persecution or famine or nakedness or danger or sword?

No, in all these things I am more than a conqueror through him who loved me. For I am convinced that neither death nor life, neither angels nor demons, neither the present nor the future, nor any powers, neither height nor depth, nor anything else in all creation, will be able to separate me from the love of God that is in Christ Jesus my Lord.

(Rom. 8:26–35, 37–9)

99

Loving Others

This is the message I heard from the beginning: I should love others.

I know that I have passed from death to life, because I love my brothers. Anyone who does not love remains in death. Anyone who hates his brother is a murderer, and I know that no murderer has eternal life in him.

This is how I know what love is: Jesus Christ laid down his life for me. And I ought to lay down my life for my brothers. If I have material possessions and see my brother in need but have no pity on him, how can the love of God be in me? I am not to love with words or tongue but with actions and in truth. This then is how I know that I belong to the truth, and how I set my heart at rest in his presence whenever my heart condemns me. For God is greater than my heart, and he knows everything.

If my heart does not condemn me, I have confidence before God and receive from him anything I ask, because I obey his commands and do what pleases him. And this is his command: that I believe in the name of his Son, Jesus Christ, and love others as he commanded us. Because I obey his commands I live in him, and he in me. And this is how I know that he lives in me: I know it by the Spirit he gave me.

I will love others, for love comes from God. My love is evidence that I have been born of God and know God. Whoever does not love does not know God, because God is love. This is how God showed his love to me: he sent his one and only Son into the world that I might live through him. This is love: not that I loved God, but that he loved me and sent his Son as an atoning sacrifice for my sins. Dear friends, since God so loved me, I also ought to love others. No one has ever seen God; but if I love others, God lives in me and his love is made complete in me.

(1 John 3:11, 14–24; 4:7–12)

100

Living in God

I know that I live in him and he in me, because he has given me his Spirit. And I have seen and testify that the Father has sent his Son to be the Saviour of the world. If I acknowledge that Jesus is the Son of God, God lives in me and I in God. And so I know and rely on the love God has for me.

God is love. Because I live in love I live in God, and God in me. In this way, love is made complete in me so that I will have confidence on the day of judgment, because in this world I am like him. There is no fear in love. But perfect love drives out fear, because fear has to do with punishment. If I fear I am not made perfect in love. I love because he first loved me.

If I say, 'I love God' yet hate my brother, I am a liar. For if I do not love my brother, whom I have seen, I cannot love God, whom I have not seen. And he has given me this command: if I love God I must also love my brother.

Because I believe that Jesus is the Christ, I am born of God, and because I love the Father I love his child as well. This is how I know that I love the children of God: by loving God and carrying out his commands. This is love for God: to obey his commands. And his commands are not burdensome. Because I am born of God I overcome the world. This is the victory that has overcome the world, even my faith. Who is it that overcomes the world? Me! Because I believe that Jesus is the Son of God.

(1 John 4:13–21; 5:1–5)

101

Disciplined in Love

In my struggle against sin, I have not yet resisted to the point of shedding my blood. I am not to forget that word of encouragement that addresses me as a son: 'My son, do not make light of the Lord's discipline, and do not lose heart when he rebukes you, because the Lord disciplines those he loves, and he punishes everyone he accepts as a son.'

I endure hardship as discipline; God is treating me as a son. For what son is not disciplined by his father? If I am not disciplined (and everyone undergoes discipline), then I am an illegitimate child and not a true son. No discipline seems pleasant at the time, but painful. Later on, however, it produces a harvest of righteousness and peace for me because I have been trained by it.

Therefore, I strengthen my feeble arms and weak knees! I make level paths for my feet, so that the lame may not be disabled, but rather healed. I make every effort to live in peace with all men and to be holy; without holiness I will not see the Lord. I ensure that I do not miss the grace of God and that no bitter root grows up within me to cause trouble and defile many.

I have come to Mount Zion, to the heavenly Jerusalem, the city of the living God. I have come to thousands upon thousands of angels in joyful assembly, to the church of the firstborn, whose names are written in heaven. I have come to God, the judge of all men, to the spirits of righteous men made perfect, to Jesus the mediator of a new covenant, and to the sprinkled blood that speaks a better word than the blood of Abel.

I am receiving a kingdom that cannot be shaken, so I am thankful, and worship God acceptably with reverence and awe, for my 'God is a consuming fire.'

(Heb. 12:4–15, 22–4, 28)

102

Love

If I speak in the tongues of men and of angels, but have not love, I am only a resounding gong or a clanging cymbal. If I have the gift of prophecy and can fathom all mysteries and all knowledge, and if I have a faith that can move mountains, but have not love, I am nothing. If I give all I possess to the poor and surrender my body to the flames, but have not love, I gain nothing. I am to be patient and kind. I am not to envy nor boast nor be proud.

I am not to be rude, neither self-seeking. I am not to be easily angered, nor keep record of wrongs. I am not to delight in evil but I am to rejoice with the truth. I am always to protect, always trust, always hope, always persevere. My love for others is never to fail.

But where there are prophecies, they will cease; where there are tongues, they will be stilled; where there is knowledge, it will pass away. For I know in part and I prophesy in part, but when perfection comes, the imperfect disappears. When I was a child, I talked like a child, I thought like a child, I reasoned like a child. When I became a man, I put childish ways behind me. Now I see but a poor reflection as in a mirror; then I shall see face to face. Now I know in part; then I shall know fully, even as I am fully known.

And now these three remain: faith, hope and love. But the greatest of these is love.

(1 Cor. 13:1–13)

103

In the Light

If I claim to be in the light but hate my brother I am still in the darkness. By loving my brother I live in the light, and there is nothing in me to make him stumble. But if I were to hate my brother I would be in the darkness and walking around in the darkness; I would not know where I was going, because the darkness would have blinded me.

My sins have been forgiven on account of his name. I have known him who is from the beginning. I have overcome the evil one. I have known the Father. I am strong, and the word of God lives in me, and I have overcome the evil one.

I am not to love the world or anything in the world. If I love the world, the love of the Father is not in me. For everything in the world – the cravings of my flesh, the lust of my eyes and the boasting of what I have and do – comes not from the Father but from the world. The world and its desires pass away, but because I do the will of God I live for ever.

I have an anointing from the Holy One, and I know the truth. And no lie comes from the truth. Who is the liar? It is the man who denies that Jesus is Christ. Such a man is the antichrist – he denies the Father and the Son. No one who denies the Son has the Father; because I acknowledge the Son I have the Father also.

I am to see that what I have heard from the beginning remains in me. If it does, I also will remain in the Son and in the Father. And this is what he promised me – even eternal life.

I am to beware of those who are trying to lead me astray by distracting me from the truth. The anointing I received from him remains in me, and I do not need anyone to teach me. But as his anointing teaches me about all things and as that anointing is real, not counterfeit – just as it has taught me, so I am to remain in him.

I am to continue in him, so that when he appears I may be

confident and unashamed before him at his coming. I know that he is righteous, and that everyone who does what is right has been born of him.

(1 John 2:9–17, 20–9)

104

Living as a Disciple

———— ○ ————

I am to keep on loving others as brothers. I am not to forget to entertain strangers, for by so doing I may have entertained angels without knowing it. I am to remember those in prison as if I was their fellow-prisoner, and those who are ill-treated as if I myself were suffering.

I am to keep my life free from the love of money and be content with what I have, because God has said, 'Never will I leave you; never will I forsake you.' So I say with confidence, 'The Lord is my helper; I will not be afraid. What can man do to me?'

I am to show diligence to the very end, in order to make my hope sure. I do not want to become lazy, but to imitate those who through faith and patience inherit what has been promised.

I am to remember my leaders, who speak the Word of God to me. I am to consider the outcome of their way of life and imitate their faith. Jesus Christ is the same yesterday and today and for ever. I am not to be carried away by all kinds of strange teachings. It is good for me to be strengthened by grace.

Through Jesus I am to offer continually to God a sacrifice of praise – the fruit of lips that confess his name. I do not forget to do good and to share with others, for with such sacrifices God is pleased.

I obey my leaders and submit to their authority. They keep watch over me as men who must give an account. I obey them so that their work will be a joy, not a burden, for that would be of no advantage to me.

The God of peace, who through the blood of the eternal covenant brought back from the dead our Lord Jesus, that great Shepherd of the sheep, equips me with everything good for doing his will, and he works in me what is pleasing to him, through Jesus Christ, to whom be glory for ever and ever. Amen.

(Heb. 13:1–3, 5–6; 6:11–12; 13:7–9, 15–17, 20–1)

105

More Practical Love

In view of God's mercy towards me, I offer my body as a living sacrifice, holy and pleasing to God – this is my spiritual act of worship. I do not conform any longer to the pattern of this world, but am being transformed by the renewing of my mind. Then I will be able to test and approve what God's will is – his good, pleasing and perfect will for me.

I am not to think of myself more highly than I ought, but rather to think of myself with sober judgment, in accordance with the measure of faith God has given me. Just as I have one body with many members, and these members do not all have the same function, so in Christ as a member of his one body, I belong to all the others.

I humble myself under God's mighty hand, that he may lift me up in due time. I cast all my anxiety on him because he cares for me.

I will be self-controlled and alert. My enemy the devil prowls around like a roaring lion looking for someone to devour. I resist him, standing firm in the faith, because I know that my brothers throughout the world are undergoing the same kind of sufferings.

And the God of all grace, who called me to his eternal glory in Christ, after I have suffered a little while, will himself restore me and make me strong, firm and steadfast. To him be the power for ever and ever. Amen.

(Rom. 12:1–6; 1 Pet. 5:6–11)

106

Walking in the Truth

I am loved in the truth – and not I only, but also all who know the truth – because of the truth, which lives in me and will be with me for ever. Grace, mercy and peace from God the Father and from Jesus Christ, the Father's Son, will be with me in truth and love.

I give the Father much joy by walking in the truth, just as he commanded me. I am to obey the command I have had from the beginning: that I love others. And this is love: that I walk in obedience to his commands. As I have heard from the beginning, his command is that I walk in love.

I am to watch out that I do not lose what I have worked for, but that I may be rewarded fully. If I were to run ahead and not continue in the teaching of Christ, I would not have God; because I continue in the teaching I have both the Father and the Son.

The Lord wants me to enjoy good health and that all may go well with me, even as my soul is getting along well. I want it to be known that I am faithful to the truth and that I continue to walk in the truth, because it gives great joy to my Father to know that as his child I am walking in the truth.

I want to be faithful in what I am doing for my brothers, even though they are strangers to me. I want to reveal God's love in the Church, and to show hospitality to others who are working for the truth.

I will not imitate what is evil but what is good. Anyone doing what is good demonstrates that I am from God.

I am to build myself up in most holy faith and pray in the Holy Spirit. I am to keep myself in God's love as I wait for the mercy of my Lord Jesus Christ to bring me to eternal life.

I will be merciful to those who doubt; I will seek to snatch others from the fire and save them; to others I will show mercy.

The Lord is able to keep me from falling and to present me before his glorious presence without fault and with great joy.

(2 John 1:1–6, 8–9; 3 John 1:2–6, 8–11; Jude vv.20–4)

107

Reconciled

I have faith in Christ Jesus and love for all the saints – the faith and love that spring from the hope that is stored up for me in heaven and that I have already heard about in the word of truth, the gospel that has come to me. All over the world this gospel is bearing fruit and growing, just as it has been doing in my life since the day I heard it and understood God's grace in all its truth.

I want God to fill me with the knowledge of his will through all spiritual wisdom and understanding, so that I may live a life worthy of the Lord and may please him in every way: bearing fruit in every good work, growing in the knowledge of God, being strengthened with all power according to his glorious might so that I may have great endurance and patience, and joyfully giving thanks to the Father, who has qualified me to share in the inheritance of the saints in the kingdom of light. For he has rescued me from the dominion of darkness and brought me into the kingdom of the Son he loves, in whom I have redemption (through his blood), the forgiveness of my sins.

He is the image of the invisible God, the firstborn over all creation. God was pleased to have all his fullness dwell in Jesus, and through him to reconcile to himself all things, whether things on earth or things in heaven, by making peace through his blood, shed on the cross.

Once I was alienated from God and an enemy in my mind because of my evil behaviour. But now he has reconciled me by Christ's physical body through death to present me holy in his sight, without blemish and free from accusation – if I continue in my faith, established and firm, not moved from the hope held out in the gospel. This is the gospel that I heard and that has been proclaimed to every creature under heaven, and of which I have become a servant.

(Col. 1:3–6, 9–15, 19–23)

108

Following the Word

When tempted, I should never say, 'God is tempting me.' For God cannot be tempted by evil, nor does he tempt anyone; but I am tempted when, by my own evil desire, I am dragged away and enticed. Then, after desire has conceived, it gives birth to sin; and sin, when it is full-grown, gives birth to death.

I am not to be deceived. Every good and perfect gift is from above, coming down from the Father of the heavenly lights, who does not change like shifting shadows. He chose to give me birth through the word of truth, that I might be a kind of first fruits of all he created.

I should be quick to listen, slow to speak and slow to become angry, for my anger does not bring about the righteous life that God desires. Therefore, I get rid of all moral filth and the evil that is so prevalent, and humbly accept the Word planted in me, which can save me.

I do not merely listen to the Word, and so deceive myself. I do what it says. If I listen to the Word but do not do what it says I am like a man who looks at his face in a mirror and, after looking at himself, goes away and immediately forgets what he looks like. But if I look intently into the perfect law that gives freedom, and continue to do this, not forgetting what I have heard, but doing it – I will be blessed in what I do.

If I consider myself religious and yet do not keep a tight rein on my tongue, I deceive myself and my religion is worthless. Religion that God my Father accepts as pure and faultless is this: to look after orphans and widows in their distress and to keep myself from being polluted by the world.

(Jas. 1:13–27)

109
True Wisdom

How great is the love the Father has lavished on me, that I should be called a child of God! And that is what I am! The reason those who belong to the world do not know me is that they do not know him. I am a child of God, and what I will be has not yet been made known. But I know that when he appears, I shall be like him, for I shall see him as he is. Because I have this hope in him I purify myself, just as he is pure.

Everyone who sins breaks the law; in fact, sin is lawlessness. But I know that he appeared so that he might take away my sins. And in him is no sin. Because I live in him I do not keep on sinning. No one who continues to sin has either seen him or known him.

I do not let anyone lead me astray. I do what is right because he has made me righteous, just as he is righteous. He who does what is sinful is of the devil, because the devil has been sinning from the beginning. The reason the Son of God appeared was to destroy the devil's work.

Because I am born of God I will not continue to sin, because God's seed remains in me; I cannot go on sinning, because I have been born of God. This is how I know who the children of God are and who the children of the devil are. Anyone who does not do what is right is not a child of God; nor is anyone who does not love his brother.

I am to show wisdom and understanding by living a good life, by deeds done in the humility that comes from wisdom. But if I harbour bitter envy and selfish ambition in my heart, I do not boast about it or deny the truth. Such 'wisdom' does not come down from heaven but is earthly, unspiritual, and of the devil.

But the wisdom that comes from heaven is first of all pure; then peace-loving, considerate, submissive, full of mercy and good fruit, impartial and sincere. Peacemakers who sow in peace raise a harvest of righteousness.

I submit myself to God. I resist the devil, and he flees from me. I come near to God and he comes near to me. I wash my hands and purify my heart. I humble myself before the Lord, and he lifts me up.

If I am in trouble I should pray. If I am happy I sing songs of praise. If I am sick I should call the elders of the church to pray over me and anoint me with oil in the name of the Lord. And the prayer offered in faith will make me well; the Lord will raise me up. If I have sinned, I will be forgiven. We confess our sins to each other and pray for each other so that we will be healed. The prayer of a righteous man is powerful and effective.

(1 John 3:1–10; Jas. 3:13–15, 17–18; 4:7–8, 10; 5:13–16)

110

Attitude towards Others

As one who is strong, I ought to bear with the failings of the weak and not to seek to please myself. I should please my neighbour for his good, to build him up. For even Christ did not please himself but, as it is written: 'The insults of those who insult you have fallen on me.' For everything that was written in the past was written to teach me, so that through endurance and the encouragement of the Scriptures I might have hope.

I will accept others, then, just as Christ accepted me, in order to bring praise to God.

The God of hope fills me with all joy and peace as I trust in him, so that I may overflow with hope through the power of the Holy Spirit.

I am to watch out for those who cause divisions and put obstacles in my way that are contrary to the teaching I have learned. I will keep away from them. For such people are not serving my Lord Christ, but their own appetites. By smooth talk and flattery they deceive the minds of naive people. I want to be wise about what is good, and innocent about what is evil.

The God of peace will soon crush Satan under my feet. The grace of our Lord Jesus is with me.

(Rom. 15:1–7, 13; 16:17–20)

111

Don't Judge Others

I accept the one whose faith is weak, without passing judgment on disputable matters. My faith allows me to eat everything, but another man, whose faith is weak, eats only vegetables. Although I eat everything I must not look down on him who does not, and the man who does not eat everything must not condemn me for eating everything, for God has accepted me.

I do not live to myself alone and I do not die to myself alone. When I live, I live to the Lord; and when I die, I die to the Lord. So, whether I live or die, I belong to the Lord.

For this very reason, Christ died and returned to life so that he might be the Lord of both the dead and the living. I, then, am not to judge my brother. Neither am I to look down on my brother. For I will stand before God's judgment seat. I will have to give an account of myself to God.

Therefore, I will stop passing judgment on others. Instead, I make up my mind not to put any stumbling block or obstacle in my brother's way. As one who is in the Lord Jesus, I am fully convinced that no food is unclean in itself. But if anyone regards something as unclean, then for him it is unclean. If my brother is distressed because of what I eat, I am no longer acting in love. I will not by my eating destroy my brother for whom Christ died. But I will not allow what I consider good to be spoken of as evil. For the kingdom of God is not a matter of eating and drinking, but of righteousness, peace and joy in the Holy Spirit, because by serving Christ in this way I am pleasing to God and approved by men.

Therefore, I will make every effort to do what leads to peace and to mutual edification. I will not destroy the work of God for the sake of food. All food is clean, but it is wrong for me to eat anything that causes someone else to stumble. It is better for me not to eat meat or drink wine or to do anything else that will cause my brother to fall.

So whatever I believe about these things I keep between myself and God. I am blessed because I do not condemn myself by what I approve. But the man who has doubt is condemned if he eats, because his eating is not from faith; and everything that does not come from faith is sin.

(Rom. 14:1–3, 7–10, 13–23)

112

A Stranger in the World

As an alien and stranger in the world, I am to abstain from sinful desires, which war against my soul. I am to live a good life among the pagans that, though they accuse me of doing wrong, they may see my good deeds and glorify God on the day he visits us.

I submit myself for the Lord's sake to every authority instituted among men: whether to the king, as the supreme authority, or to governors, who are sent by him to punish those who do wrong and to commend those who do right. For it is God's will that by doing good I should silence the ignorant talk of foolish men. I live as a free man, but do not use my freedom as a cover-up for evil; I live as a servant of God. I show proper respect for everyone: I love the brotherhood of believers. I fear God and honour the king.

I am to live in harmony with others; to be sympathetic, to love them as brothers, to be compassionate and humble. I do not repay evil with evil or insult with insult, but with blessing, because to this I was called so that I may inherit a blessing. For, 'Whoever would love life and see good days must keep his tongue from evil and his lips from deceitful speech. He must turn from evil and do good; he must seek peace and pursue it. For the eyes of the Lord are on the righteous and his ears are attentive to their prayer, but the face of the Lord is against those who do evil.' Who is going to harm me if I am eager to do good? But even if I should suffer for what is right, I am blessed. 'Do not fear what they fear; do not be frightened.' But in my heart I set apart Christ as Lord. I must always be prepared to give an answer to everyone who asks me to give the reason for the hope that I have. But I am to do this with gentleness and respect, keeping a clear conscience, so that those who speak maliciously against my good behaviour in Christ may be ashamed of their slander. It is better, if it is God's will, to suffer for doing good than for doing evil.

(1 Pet. 2:11–17; 3:8–17)

113

Serving Christ

I am one of God's chosen people, holy and dearly loved, and so I am to clothe myself with compassion, kindness, humility, gentleness and patience. I am to bear with others and forgive whatever grievances I may have against others. I am to forgive as the Lord forgave me. And over all these virtues I put on love, which binds them all together in perfect unity.

I let the peace of Christ rule in my heart, since as a member of his body I am called to peace. And I am thankful. I let the word of Christ dwell in me richly as I teach and admonish others with all wisdom, and as I sing psalms, hymns and spiritual songs with gratitude in my heart to God. And whatever I do, whether in word or deed, I do it all in the name of the Lord Jesus, giving thanks to God the Father through him.

Whatever I do, I work at it with all my heart, as working for the Lord, not for men, since I know that I will receive an inheritance from the Lord as a reward. It is the Lord Christ I am serving.

I am to be wise in the way I act towards outsiders; making the most of every opportunity. My conversation is to be always full of grace, seasoned with salt, so that I may know how to answer everyone.

(Col. 3:12–17, 23–4; 4:5)

114

God's Will for Me

The Lord deals with me as a father deals with his own children, encouraging, comforting and urging me to live a life worthy of him, who calls me into his kingdom and glory. And I thank him continually because, when I received the Word of God, I accepted it not as the word of men, but as it actually is, the Word of God, which is at work in me, a believer.

It is God's will that I should be sanctified: that I should avoid sexual immorality; that I should learn to control my own body in a way that is holy and honourable, not in passionate lust like the heathen, who do not know God; and that in this matter I should not wrong my brother or take advantage of him. The Lord will punish men for all such sins. For God did not call me to be impure, but to live a holy life. Therefore, if I reject this instruction I do not reject man but God, who gives me his Holy Spirit.

I do not live in darkness so that the day of the Lord should surprise me like a thief. I am a son of the light and a son of the day. I do not belong to the night or to the darkness. So then, I am not to be like others, who are asleep, but I am to be alert and self-controlled. For those who sleep, sleep at night, and those who get drunk, get drunk at night. But since I belong to the day, I will be self-controlled, putting on faith and love as a breastplate, and the hope of salvation as a helmet.

For God did not appoint me to suffer wrath but to receive salvation through my Lord Jesus Christ. He died for me so that, whether I am awake or asleep, I may live together with him. Therefore I will encourage others and build others up, just as in fact I am doing.

(1 Thess. 2:11–13; 4:3–8; 5:4–11)

115

He Will Do It

May the Lord make my love increase and overflow for others and for everyone else, just as ours does for you. May he strengthen my heart so that I will be blameless and holy in the presence of our God and Father when our Lord Jesus comes with all his holy ones.

I am to respect those who work hard, who are over me in the Lord and who admonish me. I will hold them in the highest regard in love because of their work. I will live in peace with others. I am to warn those who are idle, encourage the timid, help the weak, be patient with everyone. I am to make sure that I do not pay back wrong for wrong, but always try to be kind to others and to everyone else. I will be joyful always; I will pray continually; I will give thanks in all circumstances, for this is God's will for me in Christ Jesus. I will not put out the Spirit's fire; I will not treat prophecies with contempt. I will test everything. I will hold on to the good. I will avoid every kind of evil. May God himself, the God of peace, sanctify me through and through. May my whole spirit, soul and body be kept blameless at the coming of our Lord Jesus Christ. The one who calls me is faithful and he will do it.

Both the one who makes me holy and I who am made holy are of the same family. So Jesus is not ashamed to call me brother.

Since I have flesh and blood, he too shared in my humanity so that by his death he might destroy him who holds the power of death – that is, the devil – and free me from the slavery of the fear of death. He had to be made like me in every way, in order that he might become a merciful and faithful high priest in service to God, and that he might make atonement for my sins. Because he himself suffered when he was tempted, he is able to help me when I am tempted.

Because I share in the heavenly calling, I fix my thoughts on Jesus, the apostle and high priest whom I confess.

I am to see to it that I do not have a sinful, unbelieving heart that turns away from the living God. But I am to encourage others, so that neither they nor I become hardened by sin's deceitfulness. I have come to share in Christ if I hold firmly till the end the confidence I had at first.

(1 Thess. 3:12–13; 5:12–24; Heb. 2:11, 14–15, 17–18; 3:1, 12–14)

116

Comfort

I praise my God, the Father of my Lord Jesus Christ, the Father of compassion and the God of all comfort, who comforts me in all my troubles, so that I can comfort those in any trouble with the comfort I myself have received from God.

For just as the sufferings of Christ flow over into my life, so also through Christ my comfort overflows. If I am distressed, it is for the comfort and salvation of others; if I am comforted, it is for their comfort, which produces in them patient endurance of the same sufferings we suffer.

My conscience testifies that I have conducted myself in the world in the holiness and sincerity that are from God. I have done so not according to worldly wisdom but according to God's grace.

For no matter how many promises God has made to me, they are 'Yes' in Christ. And so through him the 'Amen' is spoken by me to the glory of God.

Now it is God who makes both me and you stand firm in Christ. He anointed me, set his seal of ownership on me, and put his Spirit in my heart as a deposit, guaranteeing what is to come.

Thanks be to God, who always leads me in triumphal procession in Christ and through me spreads everywhere the fragrance of the knowledge of him. For I am to God the aroma of Christ among those who are being saved and those who are perishing. To the one I am the smell of death; to the other, the fragrance of life. And who is equal to such a task?

Such confidence as this is mine through Christ before God. Not that I am competent in myself to claim anything for myself, but my competence comes from God. He has made me competent as a minister of a new covenant – not of the letter but of the Spirit; for the letter kills, but the Spirit gives life.

Now the Lord is the Spirit, and where the Spirit of the Lord is, there is freedom. And I, who with an unveiled face reflect the Lord's glory, am being transformed into his likeness with ever-increasing glory, which comes from the Lord, who is the Spirit.

(2 Cor. 1:3–6, 12, 20–2; 2:14–17; 3:4–6, 17–18)

117

Grafted In

As a wild olive shoot, I have been grafted in to the olive tree of Israel, and now share in the nourishing sap from the olive root. So I do not boast over the branches of the olive tree into which I have been grafted. If I do, I am reminded of this: I do not support the root, but the root supports me. I will say then, 'Branches were broken off so that I could be grafted in.' They were broken off because of unbelief, and I stand by faith. But I am not to be arrogant, but afraid. For if God did not spare the natural branches, he will not spare me either.

So, I consider therefore the kindness and sternness of God: sternness to those who fell, but kindness to me, provided that I continue in his kindness. Otherwise, I also will be cut off. And if they do not persist in unbelief, they will be grafted in, for God is able to graft them in again. After all, if I was cut out of an olive tree that is wild by nature, and contrary to nature was grafted into a cultivated olive tree, how much more readily will these, the natural branches, be grafted into their own olive tree!

I am not to be ignorant of this mystery, so that I may not be conceited: Israel has experienced a hardening in part until the full number of the Gentiles has come in. And so all Israel will be saved, as it is written: 'The deliverer will come from Zion; he will turn godlessness away from Jacob. And this is my covenant with them when I take away their sins.'

As far as the gospel is concerned, they are enemies on my account; but as far as election is concerned, they are loved on account of the patriarchs, for God's gifts and his call are irrevocable. Just as I who was at one time disobedient to God have now received mercy as a result of their disobedience, so they too have now become disobedient in order that they too may now receive mercy as a result of God's mercy to me. For God has bound all men over to disobedience so that he may have mercy on them all.

Oh, the depth of the riches of the wisdom and knowledge of God!

How unsearchable his judgments, and his paths beyond tracing out! It is written, 'Who has known the mind of the Lord? Or who has been his counsellor? Who has ever given to God, that God should repay him?' For from him and through him and to him are all things. To him be the glory for ever! Amen.

(Rom. 11:17–36)

118

Living a Worthy Life

I want to live a life worthy of the calling I have received, to be completely humble and gentle; to be patient, bearing with others in love. I intend to make every effort to keep the unity of the Spirit through the bond of peace. There is one body and one Spirit – just as I was called to one hope when I was called – one Lord, one Faith, one baptism; one God and Father of all, who is over all and through all and in all. That means he is over me, works through me and in me.

Therefore, I must put off falsehood and speak truthfully to my neighbour, for I am a member of the one body of Jesus Christ. In anger I am not to sin, nor let the sun go down while I am still angry. And I will not give the devil a foothold.

I will not let any unwholesome talk come out of my mouth, but only what is helpful for building others up according to their needs, that it may benefit those who listen to me. And I will not grieve the Holy Spirit of God, with whom I was sealed for the day of redemption. I will get rid of all bitterness, rage and anger, brawling and slander, along with every form of malice. I will be kind and compassionate to others, forgiving them just as in Christ God forgave me.

I am strong in the Lord and in his mighty power. I put on the full armour of God so that I can take my stand against the devil's schemes. For my struggle is not against flesh and blood, but against the rulers, against the authorities, against the powers of this dark world and against the spiritual forces of evil in the heavenly realms.

Therefore, I put on the full armour of God, so that when the day of evil comes, I may be able to stand my ground, and after I have done everything, to stand. I stand firm then, with the belt of truth buckled round my waist, with the breastplate of righteousness in place, and with my feet fitted with the readiness that comes from the gospel of peace.

In addition to all this, I take up the shield of faith, with which I can extinguish all the flaming arrows of the evil one. I take the helmet of salvation and the sword of the Spirit, which is the Word of God. And I pray in the Spirit on all occasions with all kinds of prayers and requests. With this in mind, I stay alert and always keep on praying for all the saints.

(Eph. 4:1–6, 25–32; 6:10–18)

119

Reaping What is Sown

I am blessed because my transgressions are forgiven, my sins are covered. I am blessed because the Lord will never count my sin against me.

I have no excuse for passing judgment on someone else, for at whatever point I judge the other, I am condemning myself, if I who pass judgment do the same things.

I will not show contempt for the riches of his kindness, tolerance and patience, because God's kindness leads me towards repentance.

I realise that God 'will give to each person according to what he has done'. By persistence in doing good I seek glory, honour and immortality, so that he will give me eternal life. I will not be self-seeking and reject the truth nor follow evil and so incur God's wrath and anger. There will be trouble and distress for every human being who does evil; but I shall receive glory, honour and peace for doing good. For God does not show favouritism.

For I know the grace of my Lord Jesus Christ, that though he was rich, yet for my sake he became poor, so that I through his poverty might become rich.

I am reminded that if I sow sparingly I will also reap sparingly, and if I sow generously I will also reap generously. I should give what I have decided in my heart to give, not reluctantly or under compulsion, for God loves a cheerful giver. And God is able to make all grace abound to me, so that in all things at all times, having all that I need, I will abound in every good work. As it is written: 'He has scattered abroad his gifts to the poor; his righteousness endures for ever.'

Now he who supplies seed to the sower and bread for food will also supply and increase my store of seed and will enlarge the harvest of my righteousness. I will be made rich in every way so that I can be generous on every occasion, and my generosity will result in thanksgiving to God.

(Rom. 4:7–8; 2:1, 4, 6–10; 2 Cor. 8:9; 9:6–11)

120

Enriched in Every Way

I am sanctified in Christ Jesus and called to be holy, together with all those everywhere who call on the name of our Lord Jesus Christ – their Lord and mine. Grace and peace come to me from God our Father and the Lord Jesus Christ, his grace given to me in Christ Jesus.

For in him I have been enriched in every way – in all my speaking and in all my knowledge – because the word of Christ was confirmed in me. Therefore, I do not lack any spiritual gift as I eagerly wait for my Lord Jesus Christ to be revealed.

He will keep me strong to the end, so that I will be blameless on the day of my Lord Jesus Christ. God, who has called me into fellowship with his Son Jesus Christ, my Lord, is faithful.

When I was called I was not wise by human standards, nor influential, nor of noble birth. But God chose me as one of the foolish things of the world to shame the wise; God chose me weak as I am to shame the strong. He chose me in my lowliness so that I cannot boast before him.

It is because of him that I am in Christ Jesus, who has become for me wisdom from God – that is, my righteousness, holiness and redemption. Therefore, my boast is in the Lord.

(1 Cor. 1:2–9, 26–31)

121

Speaking in Tongues

I follow the way of love and eagerly desire spiritual gifts, especially the gift of prophecy. When I speak in a tongue, I do not speak to men but to God. Indeed, no one understands me; I utter mysteries with my spirit. But when I prophesy I speak to men for their strengthening, encouragement and comfort.

When I speak in tongues I edify myself, but when I prophesy I edify the Church. Unless I speak intelligible words with my tongue, how will anyone know what I am saying? I will just be speaking into the air.

I try to excel in gifts that build up the Church. For this reason when I speak in a tongue I should pray that I may interpret what I say. For if I pray in a tongue, my spirit prays, but my mind is unfruitful.

So what shall I do? I will pray with my spirit, but I will also pray with my mind; I will sing with my spirit, but I will also sing with my mind.

(1 Cor. 14:1–4, 12–15)

PART 6

The Lord Speaks Directly to You Through the Epistles

Introduction

There follow some passages from the epistles put in the first person singular as if the Lord is speaking these words directly to you. Writing out passages in this way brings a new freshness to familiar truths and helps to remind you that all of the Bible is God's Word. It *is* the Lord speaking personally to you.

It would be a worthwhile exercise to go through the epistles passages in Part 5 and to write them out in this form: as God speaking his truth directly to your heart. I have only given you a few sections here to show you how to do this.

122

You are Light

—— ○ ——

I want you to imitate me, as my dearly loved child and live a life of love, just as I have loved you and gave myself up for you as a fragrant offering and sacrifice to my Father.

There must not be even a hint of sexual immorality, or of any kind of impurity, or of greed in your life because these are improper for my holy people. Nor should you indulge in any obscenity, foolish talk or coarse joking, which are out of place, but rather be thankful to me. For of this you can be sure: no immoral, impure or greedy person – such a man is an idolator – has any inheritance in my kingdom. Let no one deceive you with empty words, for because of such things my wrath comes on those who are disobedient. Therefore, do not be partners with them.

For you were once darkness, but now you are light in me. Live as a child of light (for the fruit of the light consists in all goodness, righteousness and truth) and find out what pleases me. Have nothing to do with the fruitless deeds of darkness, but rather expose them. For it is shameful even to mention what the disobedient do in secret. But everything exposed by the light becomes visible, for it is light that makes everything visible. This is why it is said: 'Wake up, O sleeper, rise from the dead, and Christ will shine on you.'

Be very careful, then, how you live – not as unwise but as wise, making the most of every opportunity, because the days are evil. Therefore, do not be foolish, but understand what my will is. Do not get drunk on wine, which leads to debauchery. Instead, be filled with my Spirit. Speak to others with psalms, hymns and spiritual songs. Sing and make music in your heart to me, always giving thanks to your heavenly Father for everything, in my name.

Submit to others out of reverence for me.

(Eph. 5:1–21)

123

Put on the New Self

Grace has been given as I apportioned it. I have given some to be apostles, some to be prophets, some to be evangelists, and some to be pastors and teachers, to prepare my people for works of service, so that my body may be built up until you all reach unity in the Faith and in the knowledge of my Son and become mature, attaining to the whole measure of the fullness of Christ.

Then you will no longer be an infant, tossed back and forth by the waves, and blown here and there by every wind of teaching and by the cunning and craftiness of men in their deceitful scheming. Instead, speaking the truth in love, you will in all things grow up into him who is the Head, that is, Christ. From him the whole body, joined and held together by every supporting ligament, grows and builds itself up in love, as each part does its work.

So I tell you this, and insist on it, that you must no longer live in the futility of your thinking. Once you were darkened in your understanding and separated from my life because of your ignorance due to the hardening of your heart. You were insensitive to spiritual things, having given yourself over to sensuality so as to indulge in every kind of impurity, with a continual lust for more.

You, however, did not come to know Christ that way. Surely you heard of him and were taught in him, in accordance with the truth that is in Jesus. You were taught, with regard to your former way of life, to put off your old self, which is being corrupted by its deceitful desires; to be made new in the attitude of your mind; and to put on the new self, created to be like God in true righteousness and holiness.

(Eph. 4:7–24)

124

Living by Grace

My grace has been poured out on you abundantly, along with the faith and love that are in Christ Jesus.

I did not give you a spirit of timidity, but a spirit of power, of love and of self-discipline. So do not be ashamed to testify about me. I have saved you and called you to a holy life – not because of anything you have done but because of my own purpose and grace. This grace was given to you in Christ Jesus before the beginning of time, but it has now been revealed through the appearing of your Saviour, Christ Jesus, who has destroyed death and has brought life and immortality to light through the gospel. You can be convinced that I am able to guard what you have entrusted to me for that day.

What you heard from me, keep as the pattern of sound teaching, with faith and love in Christ Jesus. Guard the good deposit that was entrusted to you – guard it with the help of the Holy Spirit who lives in you.

Pursue righteousness, godliness, faith, love, endurance and gentleness. Fight the good fight of the Faith. Take hold of the eternal life to which you were called.

You then, my son, be strong in the grace that is in Christ Jesus. And the things you have heard me say in the presence of many witnesses entrust to reliable men who will also be qualified to teach others. Endure hardship like a good soldier of Christ Jesus. No one serving as a soldier gets involved in civilian affairs – he wants to please his commanding officer. If anyone competes as an athlete, he does not receive the victor's crown unless he competes according to the rules. The hardworking farmer should be the first to receive a share of the crops. Reflect on what I am saying, for the Lord will give you insight into all this.

(1 Tim. 1:14; 2 Tim. 1:7–14; 1 Tim. 6:11–12; 2 Tim. 2:1–7)

125

Noble Purposes

Here is a trustworthy saying: if you died with Christ, you will also live with him; if you endure, you will also reign with him. If you disown him, he will also disown you; if you are faithless, he will remain faithful, for he cannot disown himself.

Keep reminding others of these things. Warn them in my name against quarrelling about words; it is of no value, and only ruins those who listen. Do your best to present yourself to me as one approved, a workman who does not need to be ashamed and who correctly handles the word of truth. Avoid godless chatter, because those who indulge in it will become more and more ungodly. I know those who are mine, and everyone who confesses my name must turn away from wickedness.

In a large house there are articles not only of gold and silver, but also of wood and clay; some are for noble purposes and some for ignoble. If you cleanse yourself from the latter, you will be an instrument for noble purposes, made holy, useful to me, your Master, and prepared to do any good work.

Flee the evil desires of youth, and pursue righteousness, faith, love and peace, along with those who call on me out of a pure heart. Don't have anything to do with foolish and stupid arguments, because you know they produce quarrels. And my servant must not quarrel; instead, you must be kind to everyone, able to teach, not resentful. Those who oppose you, you must gently instruct, in the hope that I will grant them repentance leading them to a knowledge of the truth, and that they will come to their senses and escape from the trap of the devil, who has taken them captive to do his will.

(2 Tim. 2:11–26)

126

Hold Fast to the Word

Mark this: there will be terrible times in the last days. People will be lovers of themselves, lovers of money, boastful, proud, abusive, disobedient to their parents, ungrateful, unholy, without love, unforgiving, slanderous, without self-control, brutal, not lovers of the good, treacherous, rash, conceited, lovers of pleasure rather than lovers of God – having a form of godliness but denying its power. Have nothing to do with them.

But as for you, continue in what you have learned and have become convinced of. The holy Scriptures, which are able to make you wise for salvation through faith in Christ Jesus. All Scripture is God-breathed and is useful for teaching, rebuking, correcting and training in righteousness, so that you, as a man of God, may be thoroughly equipped for every good work.

Preach the Word; be prepared in season and out of season; correct, rebuke and encourage – with great patience and careful instruction. For the time will come when men will not put up with sound doctrine. Instead, to suit their own desires, they will gather around them a great number of teachers to say what their itching ears want to hear. They will turn their ears away from the truth and turn aside to myths. But you, keep your head in all situations, endure hardship, do the work of an evangelist, discharge all the duties of your ministry.

(2 Tim. 3:1–5, 14–17; 4:2–5)

PART 7

Promises of God From Isaiah

Introduction

The promises God gives to believers are a great encouragement to them – when they believe them! In this Part we have a series of promises from Isaiah, collected together around various themes. For the most part these are direct quotations from the biblical text and will help you to see what God promises about those particular subjects. You can make your own collections of promises from other books of both the Old and New Testaments.

Of course, it is always important to take note of any condition that God makes along with the promises. For this reason it is important to consider the context of these verses. You can do this at your leisure through looking up the references given at the end of each section.

127

God's Call

I, the Lord, have called you in righteousness; I will take hold of your hand. I will keep you and will make you to be a covenant for the people and a light for the Gentiles, to open eyes that are blind, to free captives from prison and to release from the dungeon those who sit in darkness.

I will go before you and will level the mountains; I will break down gates of bronze and cut through bars of iron. I will give you the treasures of darkness, riches stored in secret places, so that you may know that I am the Lord, the God of Israel, who summons you by name.

I make known the end from the beginning, from ancient times, what is still to come. I speak thus: my purpose will stand, and I will do all that I please. What I have said, that will I bring about; what I have planned, that will I do.

I foretold the former things long ago, my mouth announced them and I made them known; then suddenly I acted, and they came to pass.

Before I was born the Lord called me; from birth he has made mention of my name.

See, I have engraved you on the palms of my hands; your walls are ever before me.

As the new heavens and the new earth that I make will endure before me, declares the Lord, so will your name and descendants endure.

(Isa. 42:6–7; 45:2–3; 46:10–11; 48:3; 49:1; 49:16; 66:22)

128

Fear Not

Fear not, for I have redeemed you; I have summoned you by name; you are mine. When you pass through the waters, I will be with you; and when you pass through the rivers, they will not sweep over you. When you walk through the fire, you will not be burned; the flames will not set you ablaze. For I am the Lord, your God, the Holy One of Israel, your Saviour . . . Since you are precious and honoured in my sight, and because I love you, I will give men in exchange for you, and people in exchange for your life. Do not be afraid, for I am with you.

So do not fear, for I am with you; do not be dismayed, for I am your God. I will strengthen you and help you; I will uphold you with my righteous right hand.

All who rage against you will surely be ashamed and disgraced; those who oppose you will be as nothing and perish. Though you search for your enemies, you will not find them. Those who wage war against you will be as nothing at all. For I am the Lord, your God, who takes hold of your right hand and says to you, 'Do not fear; I will help you.'

Hear me, you who know what is right, you people who have my law in your hearts. Do not fear the reproach of men or be terrified by their insults.

I, even I, am he who comforts you. Who are you that you fear mortal men, the sons of men, who are but grass, that you forget the Lord your Maker, who stretched out the heavens and laid the foundations of the earth, that you live in constant terror every day because of the wrath of the oppressor, who is bent on destruction? For where is the wrath of the oppressor?

I have put my words in your mouth and covered you with the shadow of my hand.

Do not be afraid; you will not suffer shame. Do not fear disgrace; you will not be humiliated.

If anyone does attack you, it will not be my doing; whoever attacks you will surrender to you.

No weapon forged against you will prevail, and you will refute every tongue that accuses you. This is the heritage of the servants of the Lord, and this is their vindication from me, declares the Lord.

(Isa. 43:1–5; 41:10, 11–13; 51:7, 12–13, 16; 54:4, 15, 17)

129

A New Thing

See, the former things have taken place, and new things I declare; before they spring into being I announce them to you.

Forget the former things; do not dwell on the past. See, I am doing a new thing! Now it springs up; do you not perceive it? I am making a way in the desert and streams in the wasteland.

The Spirit of the Sovereign Lord is on me, because the Lord has anointed me to preach good news to the poor. He has sent me to bind up the broken-hearted, to proclaim freedom for the captives and release from darkness for the prisoners, to proclaim the year of the Lord's favour and the day of vengeance of our God, to comfort all who mourn, and provide for those who grieve in Zion – to bestow on them a crown of beauty instead of ashes, the oil of gladness instead of mourning, and a garment of praise instead of a spirit of despair. They will be called oaks of righteousness, a planting of the Lord for the display of his splendour.

I will tell of the kindnesses of the Lord, the deeds for which he is to be praised, according to all the Lord has done for us – yes, the many good things he has done for the house of Israel, according to his compassion and many kindnesses.

(Isa. 42:9; 43:19; 61:1–3; 63:7)

130

Cost of Forgiveness

———— ○ ————

I, even I, am he who blots out your transgressions, for my own sake, and remembers your sins no more.

Let the wicked forsake his way and the evil man his thoughts. Let him turn to the Lord, and he will have mercy on him, and to our God, for he will freely pardon.

I will not accuse for ever, nor will I always be angry, for then the spirit of man would grow faint before me – the breath of man that I have created.

He was despised and rejected for me. Surely he took up my infirmities and carried my sorrows. He was pierced for my transgressions, he was crushed for my iniquities; the punishment that brought me peace was upon him, and by his wounds I am healed. The Lord has laid on him my iniquity. He was oppressed and afflicted for me. Yet it was the Lord's will to crush him and cause him to suffer for me. The Lord makes his life a guilt offering for me.

(Isa. 43:25; 55:7; 57:16; 53:4–10 (personalised))

131

My Support

The Lord will renew my strength because my hope is in him. I will soar on wings like an eagle; I will run and not grow weary, I will walk and not be faint.

Even to your old age and grey hairs I am he, I am he who will sustain you. I have made you and I will carry you; I will sustain you and I will rescue you.

For the Lord comforts his people and will have compassion on his afflicted ones.

The Sovereign Lord has given me an instructed tongue, to know the word that sustains the weary. He wakens me morning by morning, wakens my ear to listen like one being taught.

It is the Sovereign Lord who helps me. Who is he who will condemn me?

Though the mountains be shaken and the hill be removed, yet my unfailing love for you will not be shaken nor my covenant of peace be removed, says the Lord, who has compassion on you.

Come, all you who are thirsty, come to the waters; and you who have no money, come, buy and eat! Come, buy wine and milk without money and without cost. Why spend money on what is not bread, and your labour on what does not satisfy? Listen, listen to me, and eat what is good, and your soul will delight in the richest of fare. Give ear and come to me; hear me, that your soul may live. I will make an everlasting covenant with you, my faithful love promised to David.

Seek the Lord while he may be found; call on him while he is near.

As for me, this is my covenant with them, says the Lord. My Spirit, who is on you, and my words that I have put in your mouth will not depart from your mouth, or from the mouths of your children, or from the mouths of their descendants from this time on and for ever, says the Lord.

(Isa. 40:31 (personalised); 46:4; 49:13; 50:4, 9; 54:10, 55:1–3, 6; 59:21)

132

Promises for the Future

In the time of my favour I will answer you, and in the day of salvation I will help you.

Because the Sovereign Lord helps me, I will not be disgraced. Therefore have I set my face like flint, and I know I will not be put to shame.

Enlarge the place of your tent, stretch your tent curtains wide, do not hold back; lengthen your cords, strengthen your stakes. For you will spread out to the right and to the left; your descendants will dispossess nations and settle in their desolate cities.

All your sons will be taught by the Lord, and great will be your children's peace.

You will go out in joy and be led forth in peace; the mountains and hills will burst into song before you, and all the trees of the field will clap their hands.

If you do away with the yoke of oppression, with the pointing finger and malicious talk, and if you spend yourselves on behalf of the hungry and satisfy the needs of the oppressed, then your light will rise in the darkness, and your night will become like the noonday. The Lord will guide you always; he will satisfy your needs in a sun-scorched land and will strengthen your frame. You will be like a well-watered garden, like a spring whose waters never fail. Your people will rebuild the ancient ruins and will raise up the age-old foundations; you will be called Repairer of Broken Walls, Restorer of Streets with Dwellings.

Arise, shine, for your light has come, and the glory of the Lord rises upon you. See, darkness covers the earth and thick darkness is over the peoples, but the Lord rises upon you and his glory appears over you. Nations will come to your light, and kings to the brightness of your dawn.

Lift up your eyes and look about you. All assemble and come to you; your sons come from afar, and your daughters are carried on the arm. Then you will look and be radiant, your heart will throb and swell with joy; the wealth on the seas will be brought to you, to you the riches of the nations will come.

They will rebuild the ancient ruins and restore the places long devastated; they will renew the ruined cities that have been devastated for generations.

(Isa. 49:8; 50:7; 54:2–3, 13; 55:12; 58:9–12; 60:1–3, 4–5; 61:4)

133

His Word Fulfilled

Those who hope in me will not be disappointed.

The Sovereign Lord has opened my ears, and I have not been rebellious; I have not drawn back.

Who among you fears the Lord and obeys the word of his servant? Let him who walks in the dark, who has no light, trust in the name of the Lord and rely on his God.

For my thoughts are not your thoughts, neither are your ways my ways, declares the Lord. As the heavens are higher than the earth, so are my ways higher than your ways and my thoughts than your thoughts.

As the rain and the snow come down from heaven, and do not return to it without watering the earth and making it bud and flourish, so that it yields seed for the sower and bread for the eater, so is my Word that goes out from my mouth: it will not return to me empty, but will accomplish what I desire and achieve the purpose for which I sent it.

And it will be said: 'Build up, build up, prepare the road! Remove the obstacles out of the way of my people.' For this is what the high and lofty One says – he who lives for ever, whose name is holy: 'I live in a high and holy place, but also with him who is contrite and lowly in spirit, to revive the spirit of the lowly and to revive the heart of the contrite.'

'Peace, peace, to those far and near,' says the Lord. 'And I will heal them.'

Surely the arm of the Lord is not too short to save, nor his ear too dull to hear.

You will be a crown of splendour in the Lord's hand, a royal diadem in the hand of your God.

Before they call I will answer; while they are still speaking I will hear.

(Isa. 49:23; 50:5, 10; 55:8–9, 10–11; 57:14–15, 19; 59:1; 62:3; 65:24)

134

Righteousness

This is what the Lord says: 'Maintain justice and do what is right, for my salvation is close at hand and my righteousness will soon be revealed.'

The righteous perish, and no one ponders it in his heart; devout men are taken away, and no one understands that the righteous are taken away to be spared from evil.

Those who walk uprightly enter into peace; they find rest as they lie in death.

Is not this the kind of fasting I have chosen: to loose the chains of injustice and untie the cords of the yoke, to set the oppressed free and break every yoke? Is it not to share your food with the hungry and to provide the poor wanderer with shelter – when you see the naked, to clothe him, and not to turn away from your own flesh and blood? Then your light will break forth like the dawn, and your healing will quickly appear; then your righteousness will go before you, and the glory of the Lord will be your rear guard. Then you will call, and the Lord will answer; you will cry for help, and he will say: 'Here am I.'

This is what the Lord says – your Redeemer, the Holy One of Israel: 'I am the Lord your God, who teaches you what is best for you, who directs you in the way you should go. If only you had paid attention to my commands, your peace would have been like a river, your righteousness like the waves of the sea.'

But my salvation will last for ever, my righteousness will never fail.

(Isa. 56:1; 57:1, 2; 58:6–9; 48:17–18; 51:6)

135

Comfort my People

Comfort, comfort my people, says your God. Speak tenderly to them, and proclaim to them that their hard service has been completed, that their sins have been paid for.

A voice of one calling: 'In the desert prepare the way for the Lord; make straight in the wilderness a highway for our God. Every valley shall be raised up, every mountain and hill made low; the rough ground shall become level, the rugged places a plain. And my glory will be revealed, and all mankind together will see it. For my mouth has spoken.'

A voice says, 'Cry out.' And I said, 'What shall I cry?' 'All men are like grass, and all their glory is like the flowers of the field. The grass withers and the flowers fall, because the breath of the Lord blows on them. Surely the people are grass. The grass withers and the flowers fall, but my Word stands for ever.'

You who bring good tidings to Zion, go up on a high mountain. You who bring good tidings to Jerusalem, lift up your voice with a shout, lift it up, do not be afraid; say to the towns of Judah, 'Here is your God!' See, I come with power, and my arm rules for me. See, my reward is with me, and my recompense accompanies me. I tend my flock like a shepherd; I gather the lambs in my arms and carry them close to my heart; I gently lead those that have young.

(Isa. 40:1–11)

PART 8

The Psalms as Prayer

Introduction

For centuries Christians have valued the Psalms, not only as a rich deposit of truth, but also as wonderful devotional material. Most of the Psalms are a mixture of words addressed to God, truths about him and encouragement to put your trust in him.

In this Part I have used a selection from the Psalms, making them into prayers addressed to the Lord. This involves leaving some verses unchanged and turning other statements into prayer. It is good to learn to use the Scriptures in prayer. When you pray the Word, you know you are praying the truth. Teaching others to use the Scriptures in this way when praying has had a powerful effect on people's lives. They find themselves praying beyond their normal capacity. It helps them break out of ruts and dull routines of prayer. Prayer, like the reading of the Word, should be exciting. The Psalms are particularly appropriate for this, but other passages of Scripture, especially from the prophetic books of the Old Testament, are also good material for prayer.

The members of Kingdom Faith Church are taught to pray through passages of Scripture phrase by phrase, applying the truth first to themselves, second to the other members of the church of which they are a part, third to the immediate area which is the particular concern for a local church, and fourth for the nation. You can pray meaningfully for others when you pray the revelation of truth for yourself.

Again, you can do similar exercises for yourself, turning the Scriptures into prayer. Sometimes it is good to write these out as I have done for you in the following sections. More often you can do this spontaneously as you are praying. However, you will find it a great advantage to speak aloud when you do so, rather than simply meditating on the Scriptures.

136

A Delightful Inheritance

You are a shield around me, O Lord; you bestow glory on me and lift up my head.

To you I cry aloud, and you answer me from your holy hill. I lie down and sleep; I wake again, because you sustain me. I will not fear the tens of thousands drawn up against me on every side.

Deliverance comes from you. May your blessing be on your people.

Keep me safe, O God, for in you I take refuge. You are my Lord; apart from you I have no good thing.

As for the saints who are in the land, they are the glorious ones in whom is all my delight. The sorrows of those will increase who run after other gods.

Lord, you have assigned me my portion and my cup; you have made my lot secure. The boundary lines have fallen for me in pleasant places; surely I have a delightful inheritance. I will praise you because you counsel me; even at night my heart instructs me.

I have set you always before me. Because you are at my right hand, I shall not be shaken. Therefore, my heart is glad and my tongue rejoices; my body also will rest secure, because you will not abandon me to the grave, nor will you let your Holy One see decay. You have made known to me the path of life; you will fill me with joy in your presence, with eternal pleasures at your right hand.

(Ps 3:3–8; 16:1–11)

137

My Deliverer

I love you, O lord, my strength. You are my rock, my fortress and my deliverer; you are my rock, in whom I take refuge. You are my shield and the horn of my salvation, my stronghold.

I call to you, who are worthy of praise, and I am saved from my enemies.* The cords of death entangled me; the torrents of destruction overwhelmed me. The cords of the grave coiled around me; the snares of death confronted me. In my distress I called to you. I cried to you, my God, for help. From your temple you heard my voice; my cry came before you, into your ears. You reached down from on high and took hold of me; you drew me out of deep waters. You rescued me from my powerful enemy, from my foes, who were too strong for me. They confronted me in the day of my disaster, but you were my support. You brought me out into a spacious place; you rescued me because you delighted in me.

To the faithful you show yourself faithful, to the blameless you show yourself blameless, to the pure you show yourself pure, but to the crooked you show yourself shrewd. You save the humble but bring low those whose eyes are haughty. You, O Lord, keep my lamp burning; you turn my darkness into light.

With your help I can advance against a troop; with my God I can scale a wall. As for you, your way is perfect; your Word is flawless. You are a shield for all who take refuge in you. For who is God besides you? And who is the Rock except you?

It is you who arms me with strength and makes my way perfect. You make my feet like the feet of a deer; you enable me to stand on the heights. You train my hands for battle; my arms can bend a bow of bronze. You give me your shield of victory, and your right

* Your enemies here can be interpreted as the spiritual powers of darkness that oppose every Christian. We are to be on the offensive against them, rather than defensive. Attack is the best method of defence.

hand sustains me; you stoop down to make me great. You broaden the path beneath me, so that my ankles do not turn over.

I pursued my enemies and overtook them; I did not turn back till they were destroyed. I crushed them so that they could not rise; they fell beneath my feet. You armed me with strength for battle; you made my adversaries bow at my feet. You made my enemies turn their backs in flight, and I destroyed my foes. They cried for help, but there was no one to save them – to you, but you did not answer.

You live! Praise be to you, my Rock! You are exalted, my Saviour! You are the God who avenges me, who subdues nations under me, who saves me from my enemies. You exalted me above my foes; from violent men you rescued me. Therefore, I will praise you among the nations, O Lord; I will sing praises to your name.

(Ps. 18:1–6, 16–19, 25–41, 46–9)

138

Your Words and Your Commands

Your law, O Lord, is perfect, reviving the soul. Your statutes are trustworthy, making wise the simple. Your precepts are right, giving joy to the heart. Your commands are radiant, giving light to the eyes.

The fear of you is pure, enduring for ever. Your ordinances are sure and altogether righteous. They are more precious than gold, than much pure gold; they are sweeter than honey, than honey from the comb. By them I am warned; in keeping them I have great reward.

How can I discern my errors? Forgive my hidden faults. Keep me also from wilful sins; may they not rule over me. Then will I be blameless, innocent of great transgression.

May the words of my mouth and the meditation of my heart be pleasing in your sight, O Lord, my Rock and my Redeemer.

(Ps. 19:7–14)

139

The Lord is My Shepherd

You are my shepherd, I shall not be in want. You make me lie down in green pastures, you lead me beside quiet waters, you restore my soul. You guide me in paths of righteousness for your name's sake.

Even though I walk through the valley of the shadow of death, I will fear no evil, for you are with me; your rod and your staff, they comfort me. You prepare a table before me in the presence of my enemies. You anoint my head with oil; my cup overflows.

Surely goodness and love will follow me all the days of my life, and I will dwell in your house for ever.

(Ps. 23:1–6)

140

Your Ways

The earth is yours, and everything in it, the world, and all who live in it.

Who may ascend the hill of the Lord? Who may stand in your holy place? I can, with clean hands and a pure heart, if I do not lift up my soul to an idol or swear by what is false. I will receive blessing from the Lord and vindication from God my Saviour. Such is the generation of those who seek you, who seek your face, O God of Jacob.

To you, O Lord, I lift up my soul; in you I trust, O my God. Do not let me be put to shame, nor let my enemies triumph over me. No one whose hope is in you will ever be put to shame, but they will be put to shame who are treacherous without excuse.

Show me your ways, O Lord, teach me your paths; guide me in your truth and teach me, for you are God my Saviour, and my hope is in you all day long.

Remember, O Lord, your great mercy and love, for they are from of old. Remember not the sins of my youth and my rebellious ways; according to your love, remember me, for you are good, O Lord. You are good and upright; therefore, you instruct sinners in your ways. You guide the humble in what is right and teach them in your way.

All your ways are loving and faithful for those who keep the demands of your covenant. For the sake of your name, O Lord, forgive my iniquity, though it is great.

Because I fear you, you will instruct me in the way chosen for me. I will spend my days in prosperity, and my descendants will inherit the land. You confide in those who fear you; you make your covenant known to them. My eyes are ever on you, Lord, for only you will release my feet from the snare.

Guard my life and rescue me; let me not be put to shame, for I take refuge in you. May integrity and uprightness protect me, because my hope is in you.

(Ps. 24:1, 3–6; 25:1–15, 20–1)

141

My Light and my Salvation

You, O Lord, are my light and my salvation – whom shall I fear? You are the stronghold of my life – of whom shall I be afraid?

When evil men advance against me to devour my flesh, when my enemies and my foes attack me, they will stumble and fall. Though an army besiege me, my heart will not fear; though war break out against me, even then will I be confident.

One thing I ask of you, Lord, this is what I seek: that I may dwell in your house all the days of my life, to gaze upon your beauty and to seek you in your temple. For in the day of trouble you will keep me safe in your dwelling; you will hide me in the shelter of your tabernacle and set me high upon a rock. Then my head will be exalted above the enemies who surround me; at your tabernacle will I sacrifice with shouts of joy; I will sing and make music to you, Lord.

Hear my voice when I call, O Lord; be merciful to me and answer me. My heart says of you, 'Seek his face!' Your face, Lord, I will seek. Do not hide your face from me, do not turn your servant away in anger; you have been my helper. Do not reject me or forsake me, O God my Saviour. Though my father and mother forsake me, you will receive me.

Teach me your way, O Lord; lead me in a straight path. I am still confident of this: I will see your goodness in the land of the living. I will wait for you, Lord; I will be strong and take heart and wait for you, Lord.

(Ps. 27:1–14)

142

The Joy of your Victory

I will exalt you, O Lord, for you lifted me out of the depths and did not let my enemies gloat over me. O Lord, my God, I called to you for help and you healed me. O Lord, you brought me up from the grave; you spared me from going down into the pit.

I will sing to you, Lord; for your anger lasts only a moment, but your favour lasts a lifetime; weeping may remain for a night, but rejoicing comes in the morning. When I felt secure, I said, 'I shall never be shaken.' O Lord, when you favoured me, you made my mountain stand firm; but when you hid your face, I was dismayed. To you, O Lord, I called; to you I cried for mercy.

Hear, O Lord, and be merciful to me; O Lord, be my help. You turned my wailing into dancing; you removed my sackcloth and clothed me with joy, that my heart may sing to you and not be silent. O Lord, my God, I will give you thanks for ever.

(Ps. 30:1–8, 10–12)

143

You Hear and Answer

I will extol you, Lord, at all times; your praise will always be on my lips. My soul will boast in you, Lord; let the afflicted hear and rejoice. Glorify the Lord with me: let us exalt his name together.

I sought you, Lord, and you answered me; you delivered me from all my fears. Those who look to you are radiant; their faces are never covered with shame. I called to you and you heard me; you saved me from all my troubles. Your angel, Lord, encamps around me because I fear you, and you deliver me.

I taste and see that you are good; I am blessed because I take refuge in you. I fear you as one of your saints, for those who fear you lack nothing.

I keep my tongue from evil and my lips from speaking lies. I turn from evil and do good; I seek peace and pursue it.

Your eyes are on me because I am righteous and your ears are attentive to my cry. The righteous cry out, and you hear them; you deliver them from all their troubles. You are close to the broken-hearted and you save those who are crushed in spirit.

I may have many troubles, but you deliver me from them all.

(Ps. 34:1–9, 13–19)

144

I Trust in You

———— ○ ————

I trust in you, Lord, and I do good; I dwell in the land and enjoy safe pasture. I delight myself in you and you will give me the desires of my heart. I commit my way to you, Lord; I trust in you and you will do this: you will make your righteousness shine like the dawn, the justice of your cause like the noonday sun.

I will be still before you, Lord, and I will wait patiently for you; I do not fret when men succeed in their ways, when they carry out their wicked schemes. If you delight in my way, you make my steps firm; though I stumble, I will not fall, for you uphold me with your hand.

I turn from evil and do good; then I will dwell in the land for ever. For you love the just and will not forsake your faithful ones. They will be protected for ever, but the offspring of the wicked will be cut off; the righteous will inherit the land and dwell in it for ever.

My mouth utters wisdom, and my tongue speaks what is just. Your law is in my heart; my feet do not slip. I will wait for you, Lord, and keep your way. You will exalt me to inherit the land; when the wicked are cut off, I will see it.

My salvation comes from you, Lord; you are my stronghold in time of trouble. You help me and deliver me; you deliver me from the wicked and save me, because I take refuge in you.

(Ps. 37:3–7, 23–4, 27–31, 34, 39–40)

145

Your Plans for Me

I wait patiently for you, O Lord; you turn to me and hear my cry. You lift me out of the slimy pit, out of the mud and mire; you set my feet on a rock and give me a firm place to stand.

You put a new song in my mouth, a hymn of praise to you. Many will see and fear and put their trust in you. I am blessed because I make you my trust; I do not look to the proud, to those who turn aside to false gods.

Many, O Lord my God, are the wonders you have done. The things you planned for me no one can recount to you; were I to speak and tell of them, they would be too many to declare. I desire to do your will, O my God; your law is within my heart. I proclaim righteousness to others; I do not seal my lips, as you know, O Lord. I do not hide your righteousness in my heart; I speak of your faithfulness and salvation. I do not conceal your love and your truth from the great assembly.

Do not withhold your mercy from me, O Lord; may your love and your truth always protect me. Be pleased, O Lord, to save me; O Lord, come quickly to help me.

May all who seek you rejoice and be glad in you; may those who love your salvation always say, 'The Lord be exalted!'

As the deer pants for streams of water, so my soul pants for you, O God. My soul thirsts for you, for the living God. When can I go and meet with you? I put my hope in you, for I will yet praise you, my Saviour and my God.

You, O Lord, are my refuge and strength, an ever-present help in trouble. Therefore, I will not fear, though the earth give way and the mountain fall into the heart of the sea, though its waters roar and foam and the mountains quake with their singing. You are with me; you are my fortress.

'Be still, and know that I am God; I will be exalted among the nations, I will be exalted in the earth.'

(Ps. 40:1–5, 8–11, 13, 16; 42:1–2, 11; 46:1–3, 7, 10)

146

Have Mercy on Me

——— ○ ———

Have mercy on me, O God, according to your unfailing love; according to your great compassion blot out my transgressions. Wash away all my iniquity and cleanse me from my sin. For I know my transgressions, and my sin is always before me. Against you, you only, have I sinned and done what is evil in your sight, so that you are proved right when you speak and justified when you judge. Surely I was sinful at birth, sinful from the time my mother conceived me.

Surely you desire truth in the inner parts; you teach me wisdom in the inmost place. Cleanse me with hyssop, and I shall be clean; wash me, and I shall be whiter than snow. Let me hear joy and gladness; let the bones you have crushed rejoice. Hide your face from my sins and blot out all my iniquity.

Create in me a pure heart, O God, and renew a steadfast spirit within me. Do not cast me from your presence or take your Holy Spirit from me. Restore to me the joy of your salvation and grant me a willing spirit, to sustain me. Then I will teach transgressors your ways, and sinners will turn back to you.

Save me from bloodguilt, O God, the God who saves me, and my tongue will sing of your righteousness. O Lord, open my lips, and my mouth will declare your praise.

You do not delight in sacrifice, or I would bring it; you do not take pleasure in burnt offerings. The sacrifice you desire of me is broken spirit; a broken and contrite heart, O God, you will not despise.

(Ps. 51:1–17)

147

Your Love is Better than Life

O God, you are my God, earnestly I seek you; my soul thirsts for you, my body longs for you, in a dry and weary land where there is no water.

I have seen you in the sanctuary and beheld your power and your glory. Because your love is better than life, my lips will glorify you. I will praise you as long as I live, and in your name I will lift up my hands. My soul will be satisfied as with the richest of foods; with singing lips my mouth will praise you.

On my bed I remember you; I think of you through the watches of the night. Because you are my help, I sing in the shadows of your wings. My soul clings to you; your right hand upholds me.

They who seek my life will be destroyed; they will go down to the depths of the earth. They will be given over to the sword and become food for jackals.

But I will rejoice in God; all who swear by God's name will praise him, while the mouths of liars will be silenced.

(Ps. 63:1–11)

148

My Rock of Refuge

In you, O Lord, I have taken refuge; let me never be put to shame. Rescue me and deliver me in your righteousness; turn your ear to me and save me. Be my rock of refuge, to which I can always go; give the command to save me, for you are my rock and my fortress.

Deliver me, O my God, from the hand of the wicked, from the grasp of evil and cruel men. For you have been my hope, O Sovereign Lord, my confidence since my youth. From my birth I have relied on you; you brought me forth from my mother's womb. I will ever praise you. I have become like a portent to many, but you are my strong refuge. My mouth is filled with your praise, declaring your splendour all day long.

Be not far from me, O God; come quickly, O my God, to help me. May my accusers perish in shame; may those who want to harm me be covered with scorn and disgrace. But as for me, I shall always have hope; I will praise you more and more. My mouth will tell of your righteousness, of your salvation all day long, though I know not its measure. I will come and proclaim your mighty acts, O Sovereign Lord; I will proclaim your righteousness, yours alone. Since my youth, O God, you have taught me, and to this day I declare your marvellous deeds. Even when I am old and grey, do not forsake me, O God, till I declare your power to the next generation, your might to all who are to come.

Your righteousness reaches to the skies, O God, you who have done great things. Who, O God, is like you? Though you have made me see troubles, many and bitter, you will restore my life again; from the depths of the earth you will again bring me up. You will increase my honour and comfort me once again.

My lips will shout for joy when I sing praise to you – I, whom you have redeemed. My tongue will tell of your righteous acts all day long, for those who wanted to harm me have been put to shame and confusion.

(Ps. 71:1–8, 12–21, 23–4)

149

Your Dwelling Place

How lovely is your dwelling place, O Lord Almighty! My soul yearns, even faints, for your courts; my heart and my flesh cry out for you.

Even the sparrow has found a home, and the swallow a nest for herself, where she may have her young – a place near your altar, O Lord Almighty, my King and my God.

I am blessed because I dwell in your house; I will for ever praise you. I am blessed because my strength is in you; I have set my heart on pilgrimage. I go from strength to strength, till I appear before you in Zion. Hear my prayer, O Lord God Almighty; listen to me, O God of Jacob. Look upon our shield, O God; look with favour on your anointed one. Better is one day in your courts than a thousand elsewhere; I would rather be a doorkeeper in your house than dwell in the tents of the wicked.

For you, O Lord, are a sun and shield; you bestow favour and honour; no good thing do you withhold from those whose walk is blameless. O Lord Almighty, blessed is the man who trusts in you.

(Ps. 84:1–5, 7–12)

150

Revive Us Again

Restore us again, O God our Saviour. Will you not revive us again, that your people may rejoice in you?

Show me your unfailing love, O Lord, and grant me your salvation. I will listen to what you will say; you promise peace to your people, your saints – but let them not return to folly. Surely your salvation is near those who fear you, that your glory may dwell in our land.

Love and faithfulness meet together; righteousness and peace kiss each other. Faithfulness springs forth from the earth, and righteousness looks down from heaven.

You, O Lord, will indeed give what is good, and our land will yield its harvest. Righteousness goes before you and prepares the way for your steps.

(Ps. 85:4, 7–13)

151

Your Great Love

Hear, O Lord, and answer me, for I am poor and needy. Guard my life, for I am devoted to you. You are my God; save me because I trust in you. Have mercy on me, O Lord, for I call to you all day long. Bring joy to your servant, for to you, O Lord, I lift up my soul.

You are forgiving and good, O Lord, abounding in love to all who call to you. Hear my prayer, O Lord; listen to my cry for mercy. In the day of trouble I will call to you, for you will answer me. Among the gods there is none like you, O Lord; no deeds can compare with yours.

All the nations you have made will come and worship before you, O Lord; they will bring glory to your name. For you are great and do marvellous deeds; you alone are God.

Teach me your way, O Lord, and I will walk in your truth; give me an undivided heart, that I may fear your name. I will praise you, O Lord my God, with all my heart; I will glorify your name for ever. For great is your love towards me; you have delivered me from the depths of the grave.

The arrogant are attacking me, O God; a band of ruthless men seeks my life – men without regard for you. But you, O Lord, are a compassionate and gracious God, slow to anger, abounding in love and faithfulness.

Turn to me and have mercy on me, grant your strength to your servant and save the son of your maidservant. Give me a sign of your goodness, that my enemies may see it and be put to shame, for you, O Lord, have helped me and comforted me.

(Ps. 86:1–17)

152

Crowned with Love and Compassion

I will shout for joy to you, Lord. I worship you with gladness; I come before you with joyful songs.

I know that you are God. It is you who made me, and I am yours; I am your child, the sheep of your pasture. I will enter your gates with thanksgiving and your courts with praise; I give thanks to you and praise your name. For you are good and your love endures for ever; your faithfulness continues through all generations.

I praise you, Lord; all my inmost being praises your holy name. I praise you, Lord, and do not forget all your benefits – you forgive all my sins and heal all my diseases, you redeem my life from the pit and crown me with love and compassion, you satisfy my desires with good things so that my youth is renewed like the eagle's.

You are compassionate and gracious, slow to anger, abounding in love. You will not always accuse, nor will you harbour your anger for ever; you do not treat me as my sins deserve or repay me according to my iniquities.

Your love for me is as high as the heavens are above the earth; you have removed my transgressions from me as far as the east is from the west.

As a father has compassion on his children, so you have compassion on me; for you know how I am formed, you remember that I am dust.

You have established your throne in heaven, and your kingdom rules over all.

(Ps. 100:1–5; 103:1–5, 8–14, 19)

153

Gracious, Compassionate and Righteous

I praise you, Lord. I am blessed because I fear you, Lord; I find great delight in your commands. My children will be mighty in the land; the generation of the upright will be blessed. Wealth and riches are in my house, and my righteousness endures for ever. Even in darkness, light dawns for me because I am upright, and because I am gracious, compassionate and righteous. Good will come to me when I am generous and lend freely, and conduct my affairs with justice. Surely I will never be shaken; a righteous man will be remembered for ever. I will have no fear of bad news; my heart is steadfast, trusting in you, Lord. My heart is secure, I will have no fear; in the end I will look in triumph on my foes.

I love you, Lord, for you heard my voice; you heard my cry for mercy. Because you turned your ear to me, I will call on you as long as I live. The cords of death entangled me, the anguish of the grave came upon me; I was overcome by trouble and sorrow. Then I called on your name, Lord: 'O Lord, save me!' You are gracious and righteous; my God you are full of compassion. You protect the simple-hearted; when I was in great need, you saved me.

Be at rest once more, O my soul, for the Lord has been good to me. For you, O Lord, have delivered my soul from death, my eyes from tears, my feet from stumbling, that I may walk before you in the land of the living.

How can I repay you, Lord, for all your goodness to me? I will lift up the cup of salvation and call on your name. I will fulfil my vows to you in the presence of all your people. O Lord, truly I am your servant; I am your servant, the son of your maidservant; you have freed me from my chains. I will sacrifice an offering of thanks to you and call on your name. I will fulfil my vows to you in the presence of all your people. I praise you, Lord.

(Ps. 112:1–8; 116:1–9, 12–14, 16–19)

154

I Praise You

I lift up my eyes to the hills – where does my help come from? My help comes from you, Lord, you are the maker of heaven and earth.

You will not let my foot slip – you who watch over me will not slumber; indeed, you who watch over Israel will neither slumber nor sleep. You watch over me – you are my shade at my right hand; the sun will not harm me by day, nor the moon by night. You will keep me from all harm – you will watch over my life; you will watch over my coming and going both now and for evermore.

I praise you, Lord. I praise you in your sanctuary; I praise you in your mighty heavens. I praise you for your acts of power; I praise you for your surpassing greatness. I praise you with the sounding of the trumpet, and with the harp and lyre; I praise you with tambourine and dancing; I praise you with the strings and flute; I praise you with the clash of cymbals and with resounding cymbals.

Let everything that has breath praise you, Lord. I praise you, Lord.

(Ps. 121:1–8; 150:1–6)

155

You will Fulfil your Purposes for Me

I will praise you, O Lord, with all my heart; I will praise your name for your love and your faithfulness, for you have exalted above all things your name and your Word. When I called, you answered me; you made me bold and stout-hearted.

May all the kings of the earth praise you, O Lord, when they hear the words of your mouth. May they sing of your ways, O Lord, for your glory is great.

Though you are on high, you look upon the lowly, but the proud you know from afar. Though I walk in the midst of trouble, you preserve my life; you stretch out your hand against the anger of my foes, with your right hand you save me. You will fulfil your purpose for me. Your love, O Lord, endures for ever – do not abandon the works of your hands.

(Ps. 138:1–8)

156

You Know Me, Lord

O Lord, you have searched me and you know me. You know when I sit and when I rise; you perceive my thoughts from afar. You discern my going out and my lying down; you are familiar with all my ways. Before a word is on my tongue you know it completely, O Lord.

You hem me in – behind and before; you have laid your hand upon me. Such knowledge is too wonderful for me, too lofty for me to attain.

Where can I go from your Spirit? Where can I flee from your presence? If I go up to the heavens, you are there; if I make my bed in the depths, you are there. If I rise on the wings of the dawn, if I settle on the far side of the sea, even there, your hand will guide me, your right hand will hold me fast. If I say, 'Surely the darkness will hide me and the light become night around me,' even the darkness will not be dark to you; the night will shine like the day, for darkness is as light to you.

For you created my inmost being; you knit me together in my mother's womb. I praise you because I am fearfully and wonderfully made; your works are wonderful, I know that full well. My frame was not hidden from you when I was made in the secret place. When I was woven together in the depths of the earth, your eyes saw my unformed body. All the days ordained for me were written in your book before one of them came to be.

How precious to me are your thoughts, O God! How vast is the sum of them! Were I to count them, they would outnumber the grains of sand. When I awake, I am still with you.

Search me, O God, and know my heart; test me and know my anxious thoughts. See if there is any offensive way in me, and lead me in the way everlasting.

(Ps. 139:1–18, 23–4)

157

I Exalt the King

I will exalt you, my God the King; I will praise your name for ever and ever. Every day I will praise you and extol your name for ever and ever.

You are great, Lord, and most worthy of praise; your greatness no one can fathom. One generation will commend your works to another; they will tell of your mighty acts. They will speak of the glorious splendour of your awesome works, and I will proclaim your great deeds. They will celebrate your abundant goodness and joyfully sing of your righteousness.

You, O Lord, are gracious and compassionate, slow to anger and rich in love. You are good to all; you have compassion on all you have made. All you have made will praise you, O Lord; your saints will extol you. They will tell of the glory of your kingdom and speak of your might, so that all men may know of your mighty acts and the glorious splendour of your kingdom. Your kingdom is an everlasting kingdom, and your dominion endures through all generations.

You, O Lord, are faithful to all your promises and loving towards all you have made. You uphold all those who fall and lift up all who are bowed down. The eyes of all look to you, and you give them their food at the proper time. You open your hand and satisfy the desires of every living thing.

You are righteous in all your ways and loving towards all you have made. You are near to all who call on you, to all who call on you in truth. You fulfil the desires of those who fear you; you hear their cry and save them. You watch over all who love you, but all the wicked you will destroy.

My mouth will speak in praise of you, Lord. Let every creature praise your holy name for ever and ever.

(Ps. 145:1–21)

PART 9

The Lord Speaks Directly to You Through Proverbs

Introduction

In this Part we listen to the Lord speaking directly to us again, this time through the Old Testament book of Proverbs. For the most part these are direct quotations from the biblical text.

158

Wisdom and Discipline

Beloved, my words enable you to attain wisdom and discipline. I want you to understand these words of insight. From living according to my word you will acquire a disciplined and prudent life, doing what is right and just and fair. My words give prudence to the simple, knowledge and discretion to the young. If you are wise you will listen to what I say and add to your learning. If you are discerning you will get guidance, for you will understand my word. To fear me is the beginning of knowledge; only fools despise wisdom and discipline.

My child, if you accept my words and store up my commands within you, turning your ear to wisdom and applying your heart to understanding, and if you call out for insight and cry aloud for understanding, and if you look for it as for silver and search for it as for hidden treasure, then you will understand what it is to fear me and know me. For I give wisdom, and from my mouth come knowledge and understanding. I hold victory in store for the upright, I am a shield to those whose walk is blameless, for I guard the course of the just and I protect the way of my faithful ones.

Then you will understand what is right and just and fair – every good path. For wisdom will enter your heart, and knowledge will be pleasant to your soul. Discretion will protect you, and understanding will guard you.

Wisdom will save you from the ways of wicked men, from men whose words are perverse, who leave the straight paths to walk in dark ways, who delight in doing wrong and rejoice in the perverseness of evil, whose paths are crooked and who are devious in their ways.

Thus you will walk in the ways of good men and keep to the paths of the righteous. For the upright will live in the land, and the blameless will remain in it; but the wicked will be cut off from the land, and the unfaithful will be torn from it.

(Prov. 1:2–7; 2:1–15, 20–2)

159

Wisdom and Understanding

My child, do not forget my teaching, but keep my commands in your heart, for they will prolong your life many years and bring you prosperity. Let love and faithfulness never leave you; bind them around your neck, write them on the tablet of your heart. Then you will win favour and a good name in the sight of God and man.

Trust in me with all your heart and lean not on your own understanding; in all your ways acknowledge me, and I will make your paths straight. Do not be wise in your own eyes; fear me and shun evil. This will bring health to your body and nourishment to your bones. Honour me with your wealth, with the first fruits of all your crops; then your pocket will be filled to overflowing, and your vats will brim over with new wine.

My child, do not despise my discipline and do not resent my rebuke, because I discipline those I love, as a father the son he delights in. You are blessed as you find wisdom and gain understanding, for wisdom is more profitable than silver and yields better returns than gold. Wisdom is more precious than rubies; nothing you desire can compare with wisdom. Wisdom gives you long life, riches and honour, leading you in pleasant ways. The ways of wisdom bring you peace. Wisdom is a tree of life to you and whenever you lay hold of my wisdom you are blessed. By wisdom, I laid the earth's foundations, by understanding, I set the heavens in place; by my knowledge, the days were divided and the clouds let drop the dew.

(Prov. 3:1–20)

160

Love Wisdom

My child, preserve sound judgment and discernment, do not let them out of your sight; they will be life for you, an ornament to grace your neck. Then you will go on your way in safety, and your foot will not stumble; when you lie down, you will not be afraid; when you lie down, your sleep will be sweet. Have no fear of sudden disaster or of the ruin that overtakes the wicked, for I will be your confidence and will keep your foot from being snared.

Do not withhold good from those who deserve it, when it is in your power to act. Do not say to your neighbour, 'Come back later; I'll give it tomorrow' – when you now have it with you. Do not plot harm against your neighbour, who lives trustfully near you. Do not accuse a man for no reason – when he has done you no harm. Do not envy a violent man or choose any of his ways, for I detest a perverse man but take the upright into my confidence.

My curse is on the house of the wicked, but I bless the home of the righteous. I mock proud mockers but give grace to the humble. The wise inherit honour, but fools I hold up to shame.

Listen, my child, to a father's instruction; pay attention and gain understanding. I give you sound learning, so do not forsake my teaching. Lay hold of my words with all your heart; keep my commands and you will live. Get wisdom, get understanding; do not forget my words or swerve from them. Do not forsake wisdom, and she will protect you; love her, and she will watch over you.

Wisdom is supreme; therefore acquire wisdom. Though it cost all you have, acquire understanding. Esteem her, and she will exalt you; embrace her, and she will honour you. She will set a garland of grace on your head and present you with a crown of splendour.

(Prov. 3:21–31, 33–5; 4:1–9)

161

Guard your Heart

Listen, my child, accept what I say, and the years of your life will be many. I guide you in the way of wisdom and lead you along straight paths. When you walk, your steps will not be hampered; when you run, you will not stumble. Hold on to instruction; do not let it go; guard it well, for it is your life. Do not set foot on the path of the wicked or walk in the way of evil men.

The path of the righteous is like the first gleam of dawn, shining ever brighter till the full light of day. But the way of the wicked is like deep darkness; they do not know what makes them stumble.

My child, pay attention to what I say; listen closely to my words. Do not let them out of your sight, keep them within your heart; for they are life to those who find them and health to a man's whole body.

Above all else, guard your heart, for it is the wellspring of life. Put away perversity from your mouth; keep corrupt talk far from your lips. Let your eyes look straight ahead, fix your gaze directly before you. Make level paths for your feet and take only ways that are firm. Do not swerve to the right or the left; keep your foot from evil.

(Prov. 4:10–14, 18–27)

162

Wisdom Brings Riches

Listen, for I have worthy things to say; I open my lips to speak what is right. My mouth speaks what is true, for my lips detest wickedness. All the words of my mouth are just; none of them is crooked or perverse. To the discerning, all of them are right; they are faultless to those who have knowledge. Choose my instruction instead of silver, knowledge rather than choice gold, for wisdom is more precious than rubies, and nothing you desire can compare with her.

I, wisdom, dwell together with prudence; I possess knowledge and discretion. To fear me your Lord is to hate evil; I hate pride and arrogance, evil behaviour and perverse speech. Counsel and sound judgment are mine; I have understanding and power.

I love those who love me, and those who seek me find me. With me are riches and honour, enduring wealth and prosperity. My fruit is better than fine gold; what I yield surpasses choice silver. I walk in the way of righteousness, along the paths of justice, bestowing wealth on those who love me and making their treasuries full.

My child, pay attention to my wisdom, listen well to my words of insight, that you may maintain discretion and your lips may preserve knowledge.

My child, keep my words and store up my commands within you. Keep my commands and you will live; guard my teachings as the apple of your eye.

(Prov. 8:6–14, 17–21; 5:1–2; 7:1–2)

PART 10

The Names of God

Introduction

The Bible gives us many names by which God is called as Father, Son and Holy Spirit. I have collected some of these, but have not given you all the Scripture references. This is because for most of these names there would be numerous references for each. You can use your concordance to find these and other names of God.

As you read the Bible I suggest you watch out for these names of God, as each tells us something about his nature and character. You may like to write these out for yourself, or simply underline or highlight them in the text.

163

God the Father

God is my Lord, he has absolute authority over me. He is the Lord of Hosts. He is the Lord of Lords. He is the Lord and Judge of all the earth, and therefore he is my Lord and Judge. He is the great I AM that I AM, and all the promises he gives me are true. The Lord is holy and I am holy in him.

He is my Shepherd and cares for me. He is the Rock of my salvation. He is the Lord who provides for me. He is my Shield and help. The Lord is my banner. He is the Lord who sends me peace. He is the Almighty One, and is therefore almighty in my life.

He is my Strength. He is my Fortress. He is my Deliverer. He is the Horn of my salvation. He is my Refuge.

He is my Saviour. He is the Tower of my salvation. He is my Preserver. He is my Maker. He is my Redeemer.

He is the First and the Last. He is my Sure Foundation. He is my Husband. He is the God of Heaven. He is my Hope. He is the Ancient of Days. He is *my Father*.

164

Jesus

Jesus is the Messiah, the Christ. He is the Son of God. Jesus is the Holy One of God.

Jesus is my Lord. Jesus is my King. He is my Master. Jesus is Emmanuel – God with me. Jesus is my Saviour. Jesus is my Prophet. He is my Light. He is my Salvation.

He is my Good Shepherd. He is my Bridegroom. He is my Glory and the Lifter of my head.

He is the Word of God. Jesus is the Bread that has come down from heaven, that I might feed on him. Jesus is the Truth. Jesus is my Resurrection and my Life.

Jesus is the Door of the Sheep. Through him I have entered into eternal life. Jesus is the Way for me. Jesus is my Life. Jesus is the Lamb of God, who has taken away my sins.

Jesus is the True Vine. I am a branch in him. Jesus is the Firstborn among many brethren of whom I am one. Jesus is my Deliverer. Jesus is the power of God and the wisdom of God for me.

Jesus is my Head. Jesus is my Rock. He is the Last Adam. I am alive in him. Jesus is the Beloved, I am accepted in him. Jesus is my Peace.

Jesus is the Head of the Church of which I am a part. He is the Saviour of the Body of which I am a member.

Jesus is the Image of the Invisible God. He is Head over all principalities and powers. He is the Lord of Peace, and came to give me peace. He is the Mediator between God and myself. He is my Hope.

Jesus is the Righteous Judge. Jesus is the Mediator of the new covenant of which I am a part.

Jesus is the Apostle. Jesus is the merciful and faithful High Priest.

Jesus is Heir of all things, and I am a co-heir with him. Jesus is the Author and Finisher of my faith. Jesus is the Shepherd and Bishop of my soul.

Jesus is Just. Jesus is the Living Stone. Jesus is the Word of Life. Jesus is my Advocate in heaven.

Jesus is the Righteous One. Jesus is the propitiation for my sins.

Jesus is the first begotten of the dead. He is the Alpha and the Omega. He is the Beginning and the Ending. He is the First and the Last.

Jesus holds the keys of death and hell. Jesus is the Faithful Witness. He is the Faithful and True One.

He is the Lion of the tribe of Judah. He is the Bright and Morning Star. He is the King of the Nations.

165

The Holy Spirit

The Holy Spirit is the Spirit of God. He is Holy. He is the Spirit of Wisdom. He is the Spirit of Understanding. He is the Spirit of Counsel and Might. He is the Spirit of Knowledge and the Fear of the Lord.

He is the Spirit of Supplication. He is the Voice of the Almighty. He is the Breath of the Almighty.

He is the Spirit of the Lord. He is the Spirit of him who raised up Jesus. He is the Power of the Most High. He is the gift of God to me.

He is the Spirit of Jesus. He is the Spirit of Christ. He is God. He is Lord.

He is the Eternal Spirit. He is the Comforter. He is omnipresent. He is omniscient. He is omnipotent.

I am born again by the Spirit of God. He is the Spirit of Love. He is the Spirit of Truth. The Holy Spirit is able to inspire me through Scripture and prophecy.

He is the Good Spirit. He is the Spirit of Life. He is the Spirit of Faith. He is the Spirit of Praise. He is the Spirit of Revelation.

He is the Spirit of Promise. He is the Spirit of Grace. He is the Spirit of Glory.

He is the Wind of God. He is Living Water. He is Fire. He is Salt. He is the Oil of Anointing. He comes as the Dove.

He is the Paraclete, my Advocate. He is my Helper. He is the Witness.

PART 11

Selections From Revelation

Introduction

The concluding Part of this book gives you some more direct quotes – this time from the book of Revelation. Ascriptions of praise to God; promises he gives us, statements about his reign. And finally, the description of the River of Life.

I trust you are becoming more personally involved in the Scriptures and are learning to identify with the truths they contain. May the Holy Spirit continue to give you personal revelation of God's Word as you spend time with your Bible every day. Within the scope of this book I have been able to use only a selection of material from the Bible. Revelation awaits you on every page!

166

You are Worthy

'Holy, holy, holy is the Lord God Almighty, who was, and is, and is to come.'

'You are worthy, our Lord and God, to receive glory and honour and power, for you created all things, and by your will they were created and have their being.'

And they sang a new song: 'You are worthy to take the scroll and to open its seals, because you were slain, and with your blood you purchased men for God from every tribe and language and people and nation. You have made them to be a kingdom and priests to serve our God, and they will reign on the earth.'

In a loud voice they sang: 'Worthy is the Lamb, who was slain, to receive power and wealth and wisdom and strength and honour and glory and praise!'

'To him who sits on the throne and to the Lamb be praise and honour and glory and power, for ever and ever!'

And they cried out in a loud voice:* 'Salvation belongs to our God, who sits on the throne, and to the Lamb.'

'Praise and glory and wisdom and thanks and honour and power and strength be to our God for ever and ever. Amen!'

(Rev. 4:8, 11; 5:9–10, 12–13; 7:10, 12)

* Notice how loud the praise is in heaven!

167

Revelation Promises

He who has an ear, let him hear what the Spirit says to the churches. To him who overcomes, I will give the right to eat from the tree of life, which is in the paradise of God.

Be faithful, even to the point of death, and I will give you the crown of life.

He who overcomes will, like them, be dressed in white. I will never blot out his name from the book of life, but will acknowledge his name before my Father and his angels.

Here I am! I stand at the door and knock. If anyone hears my voice and opens the door, I will come in and eat with him, and he with me.

To him who overcomes, I will give the right to sit with me on my throne, just as I overcame and sat down with my Father on his throne.

Then I heard a voice from heaven say, 'Write: Blessed are the dead who die in the Lord from now on.' 'Yes,' says the Spirit, 'they will rest from their labour, for their deeds will follow them.'

And I heard a loud voice from the throne saying, 'Now the dwelling of God is with men, and he will live with them and be their God. He will wipe every tear from their eyes. There will be no more death or mourning or crying or pain, for the old order of things has passed away.'

He said to me: 'It is done. I am the Alpha and Omega, the Beginning and the End. To him who is thirsty, I will give to drink without cost from the spring of the water of life. He who overcomes will inherit all this, and I will be his God and he will be my son.'

(Rev. 2:7, 10; 3:5, 20–1; 14:13; 21:3–4, 6–7)

168

The Lord Reigns

I am coming soon. Hold on to what you have, so that no one will take your crown.

Those whom I love I rebuke and discipline. So be earnest, and repent.

Who will not fear you, and bring glory to your name? For you alone are holy. All nations will come and worship before you, for your righteous acts have been revealed.

Then the angel said to me: 'Blessed are those who are invited to the wedding supper of the Lamb!' And he added, 'These are the true words of God.'

'Fear God and give him glory, because the hour of his judgment has come. Worship him who made the heavens, the earth, the sea and the springs of water.'

The kingdom of the world has become the kingdom of our Lord and of his Christ, and he will reign for ever and ever.

And I heard the altar respond: 'Yes, Lord God Almighty, true and just are your judgments.'

Hallelujah! For our Lord God Almighty reigns.

We give thanks to you, Lord God Almighty, the one who is and who was, because you have taken your great power and have begun to reign.

'I am the Alpha and the Omega,' says the Lord God, 'who is, and who was, and who is to come, the Almighty.'

'I am the Living One; I was dead, and behold I am alive for ever and ever! And I hold the keys of death and Hades.'

(Rev. 3:11, 19; 15:4; 19:9; 14:7, 11:15; 16:7; 19:6; 11:7; 1:8, 18)

169

The River of Life

Then the angel showed me the river of the water of life, as clear as crystal, flowing from the throne of God and of the Lamb down the middle of the great street of the city. On each side of the river stood the tree of life, bearing twelve crops of fruit, yielding its fruit every month. And the leaves of the tree are for the healing of the nations. No longer will there be any curse. The throne of God and of the Lamb will be in the city, and his servants will serve him. They will see his face, and his name will be on their foreheads. There will be no more night. They will not need the light of a lamp or the light of the sun, for the Lord God will give them light. And they will reign for ever and ever.

He who testifies to these things says, 'Yes, I am coming soon.' Amen. Come, Lord Jesus.

(Rev. 22:1–5, 20)